TEXAS TRIVIA

REVISED EDITION

TEXAS TRIVIA

COMPILED BY ERNIE & JILL COUCH

REVISED EDITION

Rutledge Hill Press
Nashville, Tennessee

Copyright © 1987, 1991 by Ernie Couch

Published by Rutledge Hill Press, 513 Third Avenue South, Nashville, Tennessee 37210

Typography by Bailey Typography, Nashville, Tennessee

Library of Congress Cataloging-in-Publication Data

Couch, Ernie, 1949–
   Texas trivia / compiled by Ernie & Jill Couch — Rev. ed.
      p.   cm.
   ISBN 1-55853-114-9
   1. Texas—Miscellanea. 2. Questions and answers. I. Couch,
Jill, 1948–   . II. Title.
F385.5.C68   1991
976.4'0076—dc20   91-9502
                                                        CIP

Printed in the United States of America
1 2 3 4 5 6 — 96 95 94 93 92 91

PREFACE

When *Texas Trivia* was originally compiled, it became evident that many volumes could be written about this fascinating state. Texas has a colorful and compelling history based on a richly diversified land and people. Now the revised edition of *Texas Trivia* captures even more interesting facts about this exciting heritage.

Texas Trivia is designed to be informative, educational, and entertaining. Most of all we hope that you will be motivated to learn even more about the great state of Texas.

Ernie & Jill Couch

To
Joyce, Bob & Chris Powell
and
the great people of Texas

TABLE OF CONTENTS

GEOGRAPHY

CHAPTER ONE

Q. What Jackson County town was first called Macaroni Station because it served as a commissary for Italian railroad workers?

A. Edna.

◆

Q. Where was Clyde Chestnut Barrow of "Bonnie and Clyde" fame born in 1909?

A. Telico.

◆

Q. What Swisher County town has the title the "town without a frown"?

A. Happy.

◆

Q. Big Foot in Frio County is named in honor of what frontier scout and Indian fighter?

A. William A. ("Big Foot") Wallace.

◆

Q. What river flows over the rock containing the best preserved dinosaur tracks in Texas?

A. Paluxy.

Q. What river forms a large portion of the eastern border of Texas?

A. The Sabine.

Q. Who founded Salado around 1859?

A. General Sterling C. Robertson.

Q. What Palo Pinto County town is one of the leading health resort areas in Texas?

A. Mineral Wells.

Q. Measuring only 12 feet by 21 feet and honoring Elizabeth Patton Crockett, what is the smallest state park in Texas?

A. Acton State Park.

Q. What four states border Texas?

A. Arkansas, Louisiana, New Mexico, and Oklahoma.

Q. Where is the naval exhibit highlighting the World War II submarine USS *Cavalla* and the destroyer escort USS *Stewart* displayed in Galveston?

A. Seawolf Park.

Q. For whom was the town of Mercedes, founded in 1906, named?

A. Mercedes Diaz, then first lady of Mexico.

Q. What county courthouse was torn down in 1857 to settle a bet about the nesting site of a duck?

A. Grayson County courthouse, Sherman.

———◆———

Q. What city is built over a salt deposit that could supply the world's need for 20,000 years?

A. Grand Saline.

———◆———

Q. What long, shallow lagoon separates Padre Island from the mainland?

A. Laguna Madre.

———◆———

Q. In 1903 where was the first automatic telephone exchange in Texas installed?

A. Cleburne.

———◆———

Q. What is the northernmost town in Texas?

A. Texhoma.

———◆———

Q. In what community does a seven-foot-tall monument to the strawberry stand?

A. Poteet.

———◆———

Q. What town was once known as "Uplift City" because of a women's undergarment factory?

A. McLean.

Q. What Bowie County town was named for a brand of coffee popular during the mid-1800s?

A. Wamba.

Q. What town provided the granite for the Texas capitol?

A. Marble Falls.

Q. In 1943 what Lee County town became the first in the nation to have 100% of its residents contribute to the March of Dimes?

A. Dime Box.

Q. What Fannin County town received its name from a Davy Crockett campsite?

A. Honey Grove.

Q. What Carson County town derives its name from an oil company?

A. Skellytown (from Skelly Oil Company).

Q. What town describes itself as "The Big Light in the Big Thicket"?

A. Kountze.

Q. What are the four main land regions in Texas?

A. The West Gulf Coastal Plain, the North-Central Plains, the Great Plains, and the Basin and Range region.

Q. What does Amarillo mean in Spanish?

A. "Yellow."

———◆———

Q. Where did Wyatt Earp first meet his lifelong friend Dr. John H. ("Doc") Holliday?

A. Fort Griffin.

———◆———

Q. What Texas community claims to be the "Black-Eyed Pea Capital of the World"?

A. Athens.

———◆———

Q. Sounds caused by rocks expanding and contracting due to temperature changes led Comanche Indians to believe what massive granite outcropping was haunted?

A. Enchanted Rock in Llano County.

———◆———

Q. What is the smallest county in Texas?

A. Rockwall.

———◆———

Q. Who selected the name for Dallas in 1841?

A. John Neely Bryan.

———◆———

Q. How many acres did the XIT Ranch have in 1884?

A. 3,050,000.

Q. The tiny community of Ding Dong is in what county?

A. Bell.

———◆———

Q. What town has the National Mule Memorial?

A. Muleshoe.

———◆———

Q. Where was the notorious gunman John Wesley Hardin at the time he was shot in the back by John Selman, Sr., in 1895?

A. Acme Saloon, El Paso.

———◆———

Q. What city claims to be the "Chrysanthemum Capital of the World"?

A. Lubbock.

———◆———

Q. What town is known for uniquely named streets such as This Way, That Way, and Any Way?

A. Lake Jackson.

———◆———

Q. The largest university for women in the nation is in what Texas city?

A. Denton (Texas Woman's University).

———◆———

Q. What Texas community established its own circus in 1930?

A. Gainesville.

Q. In what county was the first roadside park established along Highway 71 in 1930?

A. Fayette.

———◆———

Q. "City of Mosaics" is a title recently given to what community?

A. Levelland.

———◆———

Q. In what community is the only service station a replica of a mine tipple?

A. Thurber.

———◆———

Q. At the age of 26 James Claude Wright, Jr., was elected mayor of what city?

A. Weatherford.

———◆———

Q. In 1891 where was the first Texas hospital for blacks built?

A. Galveston.

———◆———

Q. Where is La Calle del Norte, believed to be the oldest public thoroughfare in the United States?

A. Nacogdoches.

———◆———

Q. Early settlements such as Magoffinsville, Franklin, and Concordia grew into what modern Texas city?

A. El Paso.

Q. What town claims to be the "Birthplace of the Cowboy"?

A. Pleasanton.

———◆———

Q. Bovina first had what name?

A. Bull Town.

———◆———

Q. What city has the nickname "Balloon Capital of Texas"?

A. Plano.

———◆———

Q. What flamboyantly designed courthouse was called "a monstrosity" by the *Saturday Evening Post* and "an outstanding cathedral" by *Harper's*?

A. Hill County Courthouse.

———◆———

Q. What four natural elevations east of Lake Pauline in Hardeman County were a favorite Comanche Indian campsite?

A. Medicine Mounds.

———◆———

Q. Which is the largest county in Texas?

A. Brewster.

———◆———

Q. What Houston exhibit commemorates Apollo flights with a two-block-long, 32-level fountain?

A. Tranquility Park.

Q. The state of Texas contains how many counties?

A. 254.

———◆———

Q. What Hardeman County town was named for a famous Comanche war chief?

A. Quanah (for Quanah Parker).

———◆———

Q. Where was Lyndon B. Johnson born?

A. Near Stonewall.

———◆———

Q. What area of Galveston was once known as the "Wall Street of the Southwest"?

A. The Strand.

———◆———

Q. Where is the American Quarter Horse Association headquartered?

A. Amarillo.

———◆———

Q. What community is known to hunters as the "Deer Capital of Texas"?

A. Llano.

———◆———

Q. Created in March of 1848 by the state legislature, how far north did the county of Santa Fe extend?

A. To the forty-second parallel (present-day Wyoming).

Q. Where does Texas rank among the states in the production of wool?

A. First.

———◆———

Q. The National Cowgirl Hall of Fame is in what town?

A. Hereford.

———◆———

Q. In what park are four of Texas' highest peaks?

A. Guadalupe Mountains National Park.

———◆———

Q. Covering six acres, what is the state's largest farmers' market?

A. Dallas Municipal Produce Market.

———◆———

Q. The Caddo Indians of eastern and northeastern Texas consisted of how many tribes?

A. Twelve.

———◆———

Q. San Angelo was first called by what name?

A. Over-the-River.

———◆———

Q. John Nance Garner, thirty-second vice-president of the United States, was born in what county?

A. Red River.

Q. Brenham is home to what award-winning ice cream maker?

A. Blue Bell Creameries.

Q. The Alabama and Coushatta Indian Reservation is in what county?

A. Polk.

Q. What Wilson County community is named for a Polish patriot?

A. Kosciusko.

Q. What mansion built for the "Barbed-wire King" Isaac Ellwood is in Port Arthur?

A. Pompeiian Villa.

Q. "Leathergoods Center of the Southwest" is a title claimed by what town?

A. Nocona.

Q. Plano was first established under what name?

A. Fillmore.

Q. "Treaty Oak," a 500-year-old tree, stands majestically in what city?

A. Austin.

Q. Checks from oil companies inspired residents of Allentown to adopt what new name for their Ward County town?

A. Royalty.

———◆———

Q. For whom was Padre Island named?

A. Padre Nicolas Balli.

———◆———

Q. Dalhart is composed of the first syllable of what two counties?

A. Dallam and Hartley.

———◆———

Q. What city was created when the old county seat was found to be two miles off center?

A. Palestine.

———◆———

Q. What state park attracts more visitors than any other in Texas?

A. MacKenzie State Park, Lubbock.

———◆———

Q. First, Second, Third, Fourth, and Fifth Creeks are in what county?

A. Lipscomb.

———◆———

Q. Where does Dallas rank among the nation's largest cities?

A. Seventh.

Q. Where was the first YMCA established in Texas in 1859?

A. Galveston.

Q. Where did the Mennonites establish their first church in Texas in 1905?

A. Tuleta.

Q. Where is Sam Houston buried?

A. Huntsville.

Q. What notorious frontier judge is buried on the grounds of the Whitehead Museum in Del Rio?

A. Judge Roy Bean.

Q. The longest footbridge in the United States is in what community?

A. Rusk.

Q. What county and town were named in honor of the first fatality of the Texas Revolution?

A. Andrews (for Richard Andrews).

Q. Edwards Plateau is known locally by what name?

A. Hill Country.

Q. What navigational channel extends along the entire coast of Texas?

A. The Gulf Intracoastal Waterway.

Q. Texas is known by what nickname?

A. "The Lone Star State."

Q. What Texas-made fruit cake has won numerous awards and recognition for its culinary merit?

A. Corsicana "Deluxe" Fruit Cake.

Q. The four national forests in Texas are in what area of the state?

A. East Texas.

Q. What town was the first to be incorporated in Texas?

A. Nacogdoches.

Q. For whom is New Braunfels named?

A. Prince Carl Zu Solms-Braunfels of Germany.

Q. What forms the western border of the Trans-Pecos regions?

A. The Rio Grande River.

Q. What is the third largest city in Texas?

A. San Antonio.

———◆———

Q. What famous cattle trail at one time passed through Waxahachie?

A. The Chisholm Trail.

———◆———

Q. Who is credited with giving Commerce its name?

A. William Jernigan.

———◆———

Q. What Kendall County town is named in honor of a German writer and poet?

A. Boerne (in honor of Ludwig Boerne).

———◆———

Q. In what community is a fragment of Ireland's Blarney Stone?

A. Shamrock.

———◆———

Q. What European crown prince co-owns with International Paper 76,500 acres of Texas farmland?

A. H.R.H. Hans Adam of Liechtenstein.

———◆———

Q. In what town is the state's largest privately owned airport?

A. Tomball.

Q. The brand name of a threshing machine gave what 1870s Lampasas County settlement its name?

A. Rumley.

Q. What city is the state capital of Texas?

A. Austin.

Q. What city has been called "Gateway to the Big Bend Country"?

A. Alpine.

Q. Danevang community in Wharton County has what Danish meaning?

A. "Danish meadow."

Q. Where was U.S. Navy Admiral Chester A. Nimitz born?

A. Fredericksburg.

Q. Beaumont was first called by what name?

A. Tevis Bluff.

Q. The Texas legislature consists of 31 senators and how many representatives?

A. 150.

Q. What Texas town erected a statue to honor the mule?

A. Muleshoe.

———◆———

Q. Texline is situated in what county?

A. Dallam.

———◆———

Q. What Fannin County town is named for the heroic messenger of Alamo fame?

A. Bonham (for James Butler Bonham).

———◆———

Q. How many manmade ports does the Texas coastline have?

A. 28.

———◆———

Q. What is the present name of the early eighteenth century presidio of Nuestra Señora de Loreto de la Bahia del Espiritu Santo?

A. Goliad.

———◆———

Q. How many square miles are there in Texas?

A. 266,807.

———◆———

Q. What city is at the intersection of the two longest highways in the nation, U. S. 90 and U. S. 83?

A. Uvalde.

Q. The geographical center of Texas is in what county?

A. McCulloch.

Q. The name of what Wilson County town is derived from the name of a manufacturer of sewer pipe?

A. Saspamco (for San Antonio Sewer Pipe and Manufacturing Company).

Q. Reklaw is derived from what source?

A. The name *Walker* spelled backwards.

Q. The Texas Rangers are credited with originating the name of what Nolan County municipality?

A. Sweetwater.

Q. Where was the first Polish church in the nation established in 1854?

A. Panna Maria.

Q. *Alamo* is a Spanish word of what meaning?

A. "Cottonwood Tree."

Q. What cave near Boerne was named by a little boy who said, "This cave is too pretty to name"?

A. Cave Without a Name.

Q. An oil well was drilled through the floor of the National Bank of what East Texas boom town?

A. Kilgore.

Q. Where is the largest flea market in Texas held?

A. Canton.

Q. What Harris County town is named in honor of "the Father of the Port of Houston"?

A. Tomball (for congressman Thomas Henry Ball).

Q. What is the southernmost city in Texas?

A. Brownsville.

Q. What small "Victorian" community claims the title of the "Antique Center of Texas"?

A. Calvert.

Q. Twin Buttes Reservoir is in what county?

A. Tom Green.

Q. What state park contains the only covered bridge on a Texas highway?

A. Confederate Reunion Grounds State Park.

Q. The community of Cut and Shoot lies in what county?

A. Montgomery.

Q. Where is the world's largest livestock auction held?

A. Amarillo.

Q. When Mr. J. A. Money, a local merchant, declined to allow his community to bear his name, what name was reached as a compromise?

A. Cash.

Q. How many miles long is the Texas coastline?

A. 367.

Q. Star, in Mills County, takes its name from what nearby geological feature?

A. A hill resembling a five-pointed star.

Q. The name *Acton* has what old English meaning?

A. "Oak town."

Q. In the 1890s, where was the Hay Meadow Massacre trial held?

A. Paris.

Q. What town has the nickname "The Little Alsace of Texas"?

A. Castroville.

———◆———

Q. The Pecos River Bridge rises 273 feet above the water in what county?

A. Val Verde.

———◆———

Q. Between what two locations did the world's longest fenced cattle trail once run?

A. Brady and Sonora.

———◆———

Q. What Texas state park features the dreadnaught battleship *Texas?*

A. San Jacinto State Park.

———◆———

Q. Dwight D. Eisenhower was born in what Texas community?

A. Denison.

———◆———

Q. The "World's Largest Jackrabbit" is in what city?
A. Odessa.

———◆———

Q. Where in Texas did William Barclay ("Bat") Masterson serve as an army scout?

A. Sweetwater.

Q. To what name did the German settlement of New Brandenberg change its name during World War I to emphasize its allegiance to the United States?

A. Old Glory.

———◆———

Q. "The City of Live Oaks" is the title claimed by what Texas town?

A. Columbus.

———◆———

Q. Hot artesian mineral wells led to the popularity of what Falls County community?

A. Marlin.

———◆———

Q. Hardin-Simmons University is in what Texas city?

A. Abilene.

———◆———

Q. How many flags have officially flown over Texas during its long history?

A. Six.

———◆———

Q. In 1824, who built the first log cabin on the site that grew into the town of Jasper?

A. John Bevil.

———◆———

Q. For what reason was Henrietta, founded in 1857, abandoned from 1861 to 1873?

A. Nearby Indian uprisings.

Q. Where does the Dallas-Fort Worth Regional airport rank among the busiest in the United States?

A. Fifth.

◆

Q. What is the largest United States city on the Mexican border?

A. El Paso.

◆

Q. Former U.S. Senator Martin Dies was born in what Texas community?

A. Colorado City.

◆

Q. What was the previous name of Artesia Wells?

A. Bart.

◆

Q. The original plaster mold used to construct the bronze statue Iwo Jima is in what community?

A. Harlingen.

◆

Q. Where does Texas rank in population among the other states?

A. Third.

◆

Q. The Basin and Range region of Texas is more commonly known by what name?

A. The Trans-Pecos.

Q. Southwestern University, the oldest chartered institute of higher learning in Texas, is in what community?

A. Georgetown.

◆

Q. In what city is "Old Cora," the oldest existing Texas courthouse?

A. Comanche.

◆

Q. Hillsboro is nationally known for what unique 1890s structure?

A. Hill County Courthouse.

◆

Q. The Presidential Museum, displaying campaign memorabilia and dresses of first ladies in miniature, is an attraction in what city?

A. Odessa.

◆

Q. Where was a cannon used to settle a Texas feud?

A. Laredo.

◆

Q. In what northeast Texas community was Mrs. Lyndon B. Johnson born?

A. Karnack.

◆

Q. What is the greatest distance between the northern and southern borders of Texas?

A. 801 miles.

Q. What community on the Trinity River was named for a Russian naval station?

A. Sebastopol.

———◆———

Q. Texas occupies what portion of the total land area of the adjoining 48 states of the nation?

A. One-twelfth.

———◆———

Q. How many bridges cross the Rio Grande to connect El Paso to Juarez, Mexico?

A. Three.

———◆———

Q. United States Senator Lloyd Bentsen once served as judge of what county?

A. Hidalgo.

———◆———

Q. What city along the Houston Ship Channel grew from a population of 736 in 1950 to 12,773 by 1970?

A. Deer Park.

———◆———

Q. What twenty-by-eleven-foot statue is one of Fort Stockton's most popular sites?

A. Paisano Pete, the world's largest roadrunner.

———◆———

Q. Apple Springs in Trinity County shortened its name from what previous form?

A. May Apple Springs.

Q. Texas derives its name from the Indian word *tejas,* which has what meaning?

A. "Friend, friendly, or allies."

———◆———

Q. What city claims to be the "Antique Center of Texas"?

A. Calvert.

———◆———

Q. The Angora Goat Breeders' Association Museum is in what Hill Country community?

A. Rocksprings.

———◆———

Q. What Tyler County town is named in honor of a United States president?

A. Chester (for Chester A. Arthur).

———◆———

Q. For whom was Emhouse in Navarro County named?

A. E. M. House, a Trinity and Brazos Railroad superintendent.

———◆———

Q. Rancher W. T. Waggoner named what Wichita County town for his daughter?

A. Electra.

———◆———

Q. Gospel Ridge, noted for its many churches, became what present-day Grayson County town?

A. Bells.

ENTERTAINMENT

CHAPTER TWO

Q. What 1977 Waylon Jennings recording made a small Texas town internationally famous?

A. "Luckenbach, Texas."

———◆———

Q. Larry Hagman starred as Captain Anthony Nelson with Barbara Eden in what television comedy series?

A. "I Dream of Jeannie."

———◆———

Q. Sunset Carson is a native of what Panhandle town?

A. Plainview.

———◆———

Q. What Houston-born actress starred as Olive Oyl in the movie *Popeye?*

A. Shelley Duvall.

———◆———

Q. Kellyville-born actor and musician Stuart Hamblen ran for president of the United States in 1952 on what ticket?

A. The Prohibition Party.

Q. Jack Elam starred as Zach Wheeler in what comedy set in the town of Lamont, Texas?

A. *The Texas Wheelers*.

———◆———

Q. What Houston native joined the Stan Kenton band in 1974, playing tenor sax and flute?

A. Tony Campise.

———◆———

Q. What musical drama presented at Palo Duro Canyon State Park is the state's official play?

A. *Texas*.

———◆———

Q. Where was cowboy movie legend Gene Autry born?

A. Tioga.

———◆———

Q. What Fort Worth-born writer/producer wrote the screenplay for *Cabaret*?

A. Jay Presson Allen.

———◆———

Q. "The In Crowd" was a 1960s hit sung by what popular Brookshire-born singer?

A. Dobie Gray.

———◆———

Q. In what television series did Gale Storm have her first starring role?

A. "My Little Margie."

Q. What 1956 epic film starring Elizabeth Taylor, Rock Hudson, and James Dean portrayed the social, political, and economic changes of a Texas empire?

A. *Giant.*

———◆———

Q. Prior to forming his own group, Kenny Rogers sang with what well-known performers?

A. The New Christy Minstrels.

———◆———

Q. What respected show business critic was born in Fort Worth on October 2, 1938?

A. Rex Reed.

———◆———

Q. Texas natives Karl and Hugh Farr became instrumentalists in what famous musical group in 1934?

A. Sons of the Pioneers.

———◆———

Q. In what film did Larry Hagman make his motion picture debut?

A. *Ensign Pulver.*

———◆———

Q. Where was actress Dale Evans born?

A. Uvalde.

———◆———

Q. What is the real name of Dallas native "Spanky" Mc-Farland of "The Little Rascals" fame?

A. George Robert Phillips.

Q. Where was Carol Burnett born?

A. San Antonio.

———◆———

Q. In 1948 who provided the first live entertainment on Texas television?

A. The Flying X Ranch Boys.

———◆———

Q. What San Antonio native co-wrote the theme of the Dudley Moore movie *Arthur,* "Best That You Can Do"?

A. Christopher Cross.

———◆———

Q. W. C. Fields played the dad of what Corsicana-born actress in the 1935 film *The Man On the Flying Trapeze?*

A. Mary Brian.

———◆———

Q. The film *Sylvester* was shot on location in what town?

A. Marfa.

———◆———

Q. Bob Wills would turn to what Houston-born steel guitar player and shout, "Take it away, Leon"?

A. Leon McAuliffe.

———◆———

Q. Houston-born Mike Nesmith co-starred in what weekly television comedy series of the mid-1960s?

A. "The Monkees."

Q. Beverlee McKinsey and Jim Poyner starred in what NBC daytime soap set in Houston?

A. "Texas."

Q. What longtime Texas resident recorded his best-selling recitative single "Deck of Cards" in 1948?

A. T. Texas Tyler.

Q. Mansfield-born actress Ella Mae Morse is best remembered for the recording of what 1942 song?

A. "Cow-Cow Boogie."

Q. What Texas native sang the title song on the television series "The Dukes of Hazzard"?

A. Waylon Jennings.

Q. Singer/composer Roy Orbison was born in what Texas community?

A. Wink.

Q. Port Arthur native Evelyn Keyes portrayed what character in the epic *Gone With the Wind?*

A. Suellen O'Hara.

Q. For what Broadway play did Texarkana-born Joshua Logan receive three Tony awards for writing, producing, and directing?

A. *South Pacific.*

Q. What Houston-born singer/songwriter sold more than a million copies of his song "Play Another Somebody Done Somebody Wrong Song"?

A. B. J. Thomas.

———◆———

Q. In 1980 what kung fu movie starring Jackie Chan was filmed in San Antonio?

A. *The Big Brawl.*

———◆———

Q. Where was actress Gale Storm born?

A. Bloomington.

———◆———

Q. Billy Sherill and Janie Fricke teamed with what Texas songwriter to record his song "Strangers" in 1976?

A. Johnny Duncan.

———◆———

Q. What Greenville-born matinee idol won the top role in *Desert Song?*

A. John Boles.

———◆———

Q. What 1983 movie filmed in El Paso starred Chuck Norris as a present-day Texas Ranger?

A. *Lone Wolf McQuade.*

———◆———

Q. *Terms of Endearment,* starring Shirley MacLaine, Debra Winger, and Jack Nicholson, was filmed in what Texas city?

A. Houston.

Q. Plainview native Jimmy Dean received a gold record for what 1961 hit, the first of his compositions?

A. "Big Bad John."

———◆———

Q. What Houston-born actor appeared with Ringo Starr and Barbara Bach in the 1981 film *Caveman?*

A. Dennis Quaid.

———◆———

Q. What Wharton-born television newsman succeeded Walter Cronkite as CBS anchorman in 1981?

A. Dan Rather.

———◆———

Q. A backwoods village built in the swamps near Marshall was featured in what movies?

A. *Soggy Bottom U.S.A.* and *Southern Comfort.*

———◆———

Q. Where was singer Vikki Carr born?

A. El Paso.

———◆———

Q. What Houston native wrote and recorded the #1 hit "I Can See Clearly Now"?

A. Johnny Nash.

———◆———

Q. *Walt Disney Presents* starred Tom Tryon in the role of a Texas Ranger in what western series?

A. *Texas John Slaughter.*

Q. Of Crosby, Stills, Nash and Young, which was born in Dallas on January 3, 1945?

A. Stephen Stills.

———◆———

Q. What 1987 Robert Benton film was set in Austin in 1954?

A. *Nadine*.

———◆———

Q. How old was "Spanky" when he made his first *Little Rascals* film?

A. Three years old.

———◆———

Q. What name did country and western singer Hank Thompson give to his band?

A. Brazos Valley Boys.

———◆———

Q. Where was "Facts of Life" actress Lisa Whelchel born?

A. Fort Worth.

———◆———

Q. What Grand Ole Opry member is known as "The Tall Texan"?

A. Billy Walker.

———◆———

Q. Who were the guest stars in 1958 at the first nationally televised coverage of the Fort Worth Rodeo?

A. Roy Rogers and Dale Evans.

Q. In what restaurant chain did native Texan Dan Blocker have a financial interest?

A. Bonanza Restaurants.

———◆———

Q. What Texan wrote such massive hits as "Crazy," "Funny How Time Slips Away," and "On the Road Again"?

A. Willie Nelson.

———◆———

Q. What general store near Marshall has been featured in five movies?

A. T. C. Lindsey Store.

———◆———

Q. Dallas-born actress Morgan Fairchild attended what Texas college?

A. Southern Methodist University.

———◆———

Q. Waylon Jennings hails from what Texas town?

A. Littlefield.

———◆———

Q. In what daytime serial did the Dallas-born actress James Noble play Dr. Bill Winters?

A. "The Doctors."

———◆———

Q. What was the first circus in Texas?

A. The Bailey Circus (formed in 1868).

Q. In what Texas community was actress Sissy Spacek born?

A. Quitman.

Q. Where in 1985 was the zany movie *PeeWee's Big Adventure* shot?

A. San Antonio area.

Q. Ernest Tubb was fondly introduced by what nickname?

A. "The Texas Troubador."

Q. What Groesbeck-born actor appeared in such movies as *Cool Hand Luke* and *Walking Tall?*

A. Joe Don Baker.

Q. What East Texas town features a Floating Christmas Parade?

A. Uncertain.

Q. What Top 10 recording helped gain George Jones an invitation to join the Grand Ole Opry in 1956?

A. "Why Baby, Why."

Q. West Texas performer Eck Robertson was a master of what instrument?

A. The fiddle.

Q. What widely acclaimed PBS music program is produced in Austin?

A. "Austin City Limits."

———◆———

Q. In his first major role, Bing Crosby starred with what Dallas-born actress in the 1931 film *Reaching for the Moon?*

A. Bebe Daniels.

———◆———

Q. Where was country music great Jim Reeves born?

A. Panola County.

———◆———

Q. In what city are permanent art exhibits and research facilities housed in a restored county jail?

A. Albany.

———◆———

Q. What country music songwriter born in Beaumont has composed such hits as "Texas–1947" and "L. A. Freeway"?

A. Guy Clark.

———◆———

Q. What Temple-born actor portrayed Richard Nixon in the television movie *Blind Ambition?*

A. Rip Torn.

———◆———

Q. Barbra Streisand starred with what Texas-born actor in the 1976 musical *A Star Is Born?*

A. Kris Kristofferson.

Q. Lisa Whelchel made her professional debut on what television series?

A. "The New Mickey Mouse Club."

—————◆—————

Q. The set for what 1959 movie is now part of a tourist attraction in Brackettville?

A. *The Alamo.*

—————◆—————

Q. What was the name of the first game show in Texas, beginning broadcasting over KTRH in Houston in 1936?

A. "The Man on the Street."

—————◆—————

Q. Texas native Willie Nelson starred with Dyan Cannon in what 1980 movie?

A. *Honeysuckle Rose.*

—————◆—————

Q. What Ennis-born producer/director was the Emmy award winning director of "The Dinah Shore Chevy Show"?

A. Bob Banner.

—————◆—————

Q. What San Benito-born country music performer was born Baldemar G. Huerta?

A. Freddy Fender.

—————◆—————

Q. In what county is the Ewing's South Fork Ranch located?

A. Braddock.

Q. What legendary Texas-born songwriter listed among his many compositions "This Ole House" and "It Is No Secret"?

A. Stuart Hamblen.

———◆———

Q. The Grapevine Opry building was used in the filming of what 1983 movie starring Robert Duvall?

A. *Tender Mercies*.

———◆———

Q. What Texas native was the first country artist to record on Capitol Records?

A. Tex Ritter.

———◆———

Q. In 1979 what PBS science fiction movie was shot at the Tandy Center and the Fort Worth Water Gardens?

A. *The Lathe of Heaven*.

———◆———

Q. What Mexia-born musician composed and conducted his arrangements on such shows as "The Hollywood Palace," "The Bob Hope Show," and "The Milton Berle Show"?

A. Les Baxter.

———◆———

Q. Actress Debbie Reynolds was born in what city?
A. El Paso.

———◆———

Q. In what state park is the outdoor drama *Texas* performed?

A. Palo Duro Canyon.

Q. What musical duo first joined forces in a rock group called the Champs?

A. Seals & Croft.

Q. Dean Martin had a smash hit recording in 1965 bearing the name of what Texas city?

A. Houston.

Q. What 1983 CBS series starring Jim Metzler, Alec Baldwin, and Shelley Hack focused on three physicians working in a small Texas town?

A. "Cutter to Houston."

Q. Actress/choreographer/director Valerie Bettis was born in what city?

A. Houston.

Q. What was the name of the first black independent record label in the South?

A. Peacock Records, Houston.

Q. "Windows on Main Street," a 1961–62 television series, showcased what former Dallas resident as Robert Young's leading lady?

A. Constance Moore.

Q. In what museum are the remains of "Big Jim," a horned toad who was airmailed to fourteen different cities in 1938?

A. Heritage Museum, Big Spring.

Q. Abilene native Ann Wedgeworth portrayed which character in the daytime serial "Somerset"?

A. Lahoma Lucas.

---◆---

Q. Country singer Don Williams was born in what Texas community?

A. Floydada.

---◆---

Q. What 1983 movie was filmed in part of Houston, with Burt Lancaster playing an eccentric oil billionaire?

A. *Local Hero*.

---◆---

Q. What Dallas-born cinematographer help create such films as *Lady Sings the Blues*, *The Bad News Bears*, and *Norma Rae*?

A. John A. Alonzo.

---◆---

Q. In 1980 Texas-born Sissy Spacek received an Academy Award as Best Actress for what film?

A. *Coal Miner's Daughter*.

---◆---

Q. In the 1970s Johnny Cash recorded the chart topper "Old Chunk of Coal" written by what Corsicana native?

A. Billy Joe Shaver.

---◆---

Q. Tex Ritter enrolled at the University of Texas to study for what profession?

A. Law.

Q. Jimmy Stewart and June Allyson starred in what film portraying the life of a Celeste-born major league ball player?

A. *The Monty Stratton Story*.

Q. What author is noted for his reviews of drive-in movies?

A. Joe Bob Briggs (aka John Bloom).

Q. Comedian Steve Martin is a native of what Texas city?

A. Waco.

Q. What 1965 song recorded by Ernest Tubb sold one million copies?

A. "Walking the Floor Over You."

Q. What former model born in Alice appeared in such films as *The Way We Were* and *Moonraker*?

A. Lois Chiles.

Q. What Houston-born multi-talented singer/musician married singer Rosanne Cash in 1979?

A. Rodney Crowell.

Q. San Saba native Tommy Lee Jones portrayed what mysterious billionaire in a 1977 TV movie?

A. Howard Hughes (in *The Amazing Howard Hughes*).

Q. Gladys City, a replica of a 1901 oil town, is in what Texas city?

A. Beaumont.

———◆———

Q. What Pulitzer-prize winning novel by Larry McMurtry was made into an award-winning television mini-series?

A. *Lonesome Dove.*

———◆———

Q. *Strange Intruder* (1956) was the last film made by what Fort Sam Houston-born actress?

A. Ann Harding.

———◆———

Q. Mac Davis is a native of what Texas town?

A. Lubbock.

———◆———

Q. Texas native Susan Howard joined the "Dallas" cast in 1979, playing what character?

A. Donna Culver, who married Ray Krebbs.

———◆———

Q. What Kemp native wrote the award winning song "One Day At A Time"?

A. Marijohn Wilkin.

———◆———

Q. What Fort Worth-born musician was a Glenn Miller soloist from 1938 to 1942?

A. Tex Beneke.

Q. Former Miss America Phyllis George was born in what Texas community?

A. Denton.

◆

Q. What Garland establishment provided hats for "J. R. Ewing"?

A. Resistol Hat Factory.

◆

Q. WBAP-TV, the state's first television station, began operation in 1947 in what city?

A. Fort Worth.

◆

Q. What Aguilares-born actor appeared in such films as *Rio Bravo, The Love Bug,* and *Support Your Local Gunfighter?*

A. Pedro Gonzalez-Gonzalez.

◆

Q. Jimmy Dean and his group, the Texas Wildcats, first gained national recognition with what song?

A. "Bummin' Around."

◆

Q. What Texas-born actress played Casey, an I.M.F. agent, on the television adventure series "Mission Impossible"?

A. Lynda Day George.

◆

Q. Jimmy Webb wrote what 1969 chart topper for singer Glen Campbell?

A. "Galveston."

Q. Audie Murphy starred in what movie based on Stephen Crane's Civil War short story?

A. *Red Badge of Courage*.

———◆———

Q. What recording brought Anson-born Jeannie C. Riley to instant notoriety?

A. "Harper Valley PTA" (written by Tom T. Hall).

———◆———

Q. Where was actor Larry Hagman born?
A. Weatherford.

———◆———

Q. What Dallas-born actor portrayed Charles Manson in the 1976 movie *Helter Skelter?*

A. Steve Railsback.

———◆———

Q. The talents of what Sabina-born country singer were first discovered while he was jailed as a teenager for goat-rustling?

A. Johnny Rodriguez.

———◆———

Q. What Texas native played the male chauvinist boss in the comedy film *Nine to Five?*

A. Dabney Coleman.

———◆———

Q. What Texas-born celebrity was co-host of the CBS "NFL Today" show?

A. Phyllis George.

Q. What 1983 movie filmed in Dallas starred Meryl Streep, Cher, and Kurt Russell?

A. *Silkwood*.

Q. Marshall native Susan Howard played the wife of actor Barry Newman in what 1970s television crime drama?

A. "Petrocelli."

Q. Steve Martin received a Grammy in 1978 for what comedy album?

A. *A Wild and Crazy Guy*.

Q. Veteran band leader Bob Wills pioneered what style of country music?

A. Western swing.

Q. What famous country music singing sisters were born in Seminole?

A. Tanya Tucker and La Costa.

Q. Outdoor scenes for what movie were shot in the southern community of Roma?

A. *Viva Zapata*.

Q. What San Antonio resident is the singer of such hits as "Amarillo by Morning"?

A. George Strait.

Q. Lubbock-born rock star Buddy Holly hit number one on the charts with what 1957 recording?

A. "That'll Be The Day."

———◆———

Q. What Houston-born actress/dancer gained instant popularity in the television show "Fame"?

A. Debbie Allen.

———◆———

Q. In 1978 what song became Houston-born Barbara Mandrell's first number one hit?

A. "Sleeping Single In A Double Bed."

———◆———

Q. What Texas native directed *The Funhouse* in 1981 and *Poltergeist* in 1982?

A. Tobe Hooper.

———◆———

Q. Willie Nelson composed what top-of-the-charts single for Faron Young in the early sixties?

A. "Hello Walls."

———◆———

Q. What Prairie View native played bass in the Cannonball Adderley quintet the last seven years of the group's existence?

A. Walter M. Booker, Jr.

———◆———

Q. In 1979 what El Paso-born writer/producer created *Star Trek*?

A. Gene Roddenberry.

Q. What Houston-born actor/writer/producer had the title role in the 1967 Broadway show *Trial of Lee Harvey Oswald?*

A. Peter Masterson.

———◆———

Q. In what Texas community did Roy Orbison have his own radio show while still in high school?

A. Vernon.

———◆———

Q. What "New Traditionalist" country singer is known for such hits as "San Antonio Girl"?

A. Steve Earle.

———◆———

Q. What Texas-born writer/actor co-wrote and starred in the 1979 Broadway production of *The Best Little Whorehouse in Texas?*

A. Larry L. King.

———◆———

Q. As a writer and performer Tex Ritter pioneered what legendary radio program?

A. The original "Lone Ranger" series.

———◆———

Q. Where was actress Sandy Duncan born?

A. Henderson.

———◆———

Q. What television series starring Benji the dog was videotaped in Dallas?

A. "Benji, Zax, and The Alien Prince."

Q. For what song did Brownsville native Kris Kristofferson receive a Grammy in 1971?

A. "Help Me Make It Through the Night."

———◆———

Q. Texas-born playwright Horton Foote authored what 1956 novel?

A. *The Chase*.

———◆———

Q. In what film did Debbie Reynolds make her screen debut in 1948?

A. *June Bride*.

———◆———

Q. What 1927 movie shot around Fort Sam Houston in 1926 became the first recipient of an "Oscar"?

A. *Wings*.

———◆———

Q. What Abilene-born musician composed for "The Andy Williams Show," "Petula Clark Show," and "Glen Campbell Show"?

A. Mason Williams.

———◆———

Q. What was the name of Gene Autry's horse?

A. Champion.

———◆———

Q. Tanya Tucker began her national singing career with what smash recording?

A. "Delta Dawn."

Q. Where was model/actress Jaclyn Smith born?

A. Houston.

———◆———

Q. What legendary country music pioneer maintained a home in Kerrville?

A. Jimmie Rodgers.

———◆———

Q. Thomas A. Edison signed what Jefferson-born singer to the Edison Diamond Disc recording label with his first release being "Can't Yo Hea'h Me Calling Caroline"?

A. Vernon Dalhart.

———◆———

Q. What 1984 movie filmed in Dallas starred Sally Field as a sheriff's widow?

A. *Places in the Heart.*

———◆———

Q. Gary Busey starred in what film portraying the life of a rock-n-roll legend?

A. *The Buddy Holly Story.*

———◆———

Q. What Roger Miller song won four Grammys, including Country Song of the Year in 1964?

A. "Dang Me."

———◆———

Q. Farrah Fawcett played a private detective named Jill Munroe on what crime drama television series?

A. "Charlie's Angels."

Q. Amarillo-born actress Carolyn Jones played what character on the comedy series "The Addams Family"?

A. Morticia.

———◆———

Q. What Mac Davis song has been recorded by over fifty artists?

A. "I Believe in Music."

———◆———

Q. Where was actress Lynda Day George born?

A. San Marcos.

———◆———

Q. Before joining the Oak Ridge Boys, what singer was a deejay at KPLT radio in Paris?

A. Duane Allen.

———◆———

Q. What Amarillo-born actress made her screen debut in *Something to Shout About?*

A. Cyd Charisse.

———◆———

Q. What Roy Orbison recording sold over seven million copies in the 1960s?

A. "Pretty Woman."

———◆———

Q. Dale Evans was known by what title on the television series "The Roy Rogers and Dale Evans Show"?

A. Queen of the West.

Q. What famous Texas-born director acted in the film *Love & Money* during the last year of his life?

A. King Vidor.

Q. Dabney Coleman played what character on the television series "Mary Hartman, Mary Hartman"?

A. Merle Jeeter, the mayor.

Q. In what Bowie County community was actor Dan Blocker born?

A. DeKalb.

Q. Morgan Fairchild played the character Jennifer Phillips on what television soap opera?

A. "Search For Tomorrow."

Q. What Larry McMurtry novel was made into a 1971 movie starring Timothy Bottoms, Cybill Shepherd, and Jeff Bridges?

A. *The Last Picture Show*.

Q. What filmmaker shot his *The Whole Shootin' Match* for a reported $15,000?

A. Eagle Pennell.

Q. What Waco-born leading lady of the forties appeared in the film *House of Frankenstein* in 1945?

A. Anne Gwynne.

Q. In what film did Mac Davis make his successful movie debut as a pro football player?

A. *North Dallas 40.*

——————◆——————

Q. Country music legend George Jones was born in what Texas town?

A. Saratoga.

——————◆——————

Q. What Fort Worth-born leading lady of the fifties has appeared in numerous films, including *The Carpetbaggers* (1964) and *The Sons of Katie Elder* (1965)?

A. Martha Hyer.

——————◆——————

Q. Her appearances on what television show garnered Carol Burnett her first Emmy?

A. "The Garry Moore Show."

——————◆——————

Q. Jaclyn Smith portrayed one of America's first ladies in what made-for-television movie?

A. *Jacqueline Bouvier Kennedy.*

——————◆——————

Q. "She Wakes Me Every Morning" was a late 1970s hit for what Cass County-born singer/songwriter?

A. Nat Stuckey.

——————◆——————

Q. What Duncanville resident was crowned National Disco Champion in 1978?

A. Bruce Kackler.

Q. What hit song made Texan Jim Reeves an international star in 1960?

A. "He'll Have To Go."

◆

Q. Milton Berle hosted what 60-minute variety show sponsored by Texaco from 1948 to 1953?

A. "The Texaco Star Theatre."

◆

Q. What rock star once worked for the Gates Memorial Library in Port Arthur?

A. Janis Joplin.

◆

Q. Galveston native Katherine Helmond portrayed what character on the television comedy series "Soap"?

A. Jessica Tate.

◆

Q. What Houston-born actress starred with actor Nick Nolte in the 1984 film *Teachers?*

A. JoBeth Williams.

◆

Q. The hat worn by Don Williams on and off stage was designed for him to wear on the set of what Burt Reynolds movie?

A. *W. W. and the Dixie Dancekings.*

◆

Q. What Nederland-born actress appeared in *Day of the Dolphin* and *The Choirboys?*

A. Phyllis Davis.

Q. Larry Gatlin is a native of what Texas community?

A. Seminole.

———◆———

Q. Warner Brothers shot what film in 1981 in Nacogdoches County starring James Garner and Joan Hackett?

A. *The Long Hot Summer of George Adams*.

———◆———

Q. What famous Houston-born motion picture executive became president of the Motion Picture Association of America in 1966?

A. Jack Valenti.

———◆———

Q. Dallas native Michael Murphey received a gold record for what song in 1975?

A. "Wildfire."

———◆———

Q. What Corpus Christi-filmed movie starred Sissy Spacek as the only switchboard operator in a Texas town?

A. *Raggedy Man*.

———◆———

Q. Wharton-born playwright Horton Foote received an Academy Award for what 1962 screenplay?

A. *To Kill a Mockingbird*.

———◆———

Q. What Sidney-born musician won the Texas state fiddling championship at the age of nine?

A. Jim Seals.

Q. What Texas-born actress won a 1955 Emmy for the television production of *Peter Pan?*

A. Mary Martin.

Q. In 1979 what Waxahachie-born writer/director received Oscar awards for *Kramer vs. Kramer?*

A. Robert Benton.

Q. What Dallas-born rocker received a gold record for his 1973 recording of "The Joker"?

A. Steve Miller.

Q. Gene Autry starred in how many musical Western feature movies?

A. Eighty-eight.

Q. What is the original name of actress Cyd Charisse?

A. Tula Ellice Finklea.

Q. What Synder-born actor won an Emmy in 1980 for his television performance in *Guyana Tragedy–The Story of Jim Jones?*

A. Powers Boothe.

Q. What country music writer/performer born in Gainsville earned a diploma in agriculture from West Texas State University?

A. Red Steagall.

Q. What Houston-born actress/dancer/singer starred with Mickey Rooney in the Broadway hit *Sugar Babies?*

A. Ann Miller.

◆

Q. Waylon Jennings was a member of what rock-and-roll band in the 1950s?

A. The Crickets (Buddy Holly's band).

◆

Q. On what television crime drama did Huntsville-born Steve Forrest play Lieutenant Hondo Harrelson?

A. "S.W.A.T."

◆

Q. What Big Spring native appeared in the film *Tender Mercies,* in television's "Eight Is Enough," and Broadway's *Cats?*

A. Betty Buckley.

◆

Q. In what town is the Bob Wills Museum?

A. Turkey.

◆

Q. What Dallas-born actor co-starred with Glynnis O'Connor in the film *Ode to Billie Joe?*

A. Robby Benson.

◆

Q. Texas-born actress Phyllis Davis played Beatrice, a show girl, in what television crime drama series?

A. "Vega$."

Q. In 1980 and 1981 what George Jones recording won numerous awards, including Song of the Year?

A. "He Stopped Loving Her Today."

———◆———

Q. What former model born in San Antonio appeared in the films *The Interns* (1962) and *Chamber of Horrors* (1966)?

A. Suzy Parker.

———◆———

Q. What city was the birthplace of jazz great Jack Teagarden?

A. Vernon.

———◆———

Q. What Hereford-born actor starred as Tarzan in the NBC series "Tarzan" in 1966?

A. Ron Ely (Ronald Pierce).

———◆———

Q. David Hansen was a character played by what Houston-born actor in the crime drama *Storefront Lawyers*?

A. Robert Foxworth.

———◆———

Q. What television western detailed the investigations of two Texas Rangers Jace Pearson and Clay Morgan?

A. *Tales of the Texas Rangers*.

———◆———

Q. Where was Grand Ole Opry member Justin Tubb born?

A. San Antonio.

Q. In the 1965 Woody Allen film *What's New Pussycat,* what San Antonio-born actress pursued a fashion-magazine editor played by Peter O'Toole?

A. Paula Prentiss.

———◆———

Q. What Groveton native became well-known for his impersonations of such performers as Elvis Presley, Ernest Tubb, Walter Brennan, and Johnny Cash?

A. Jacky Ward.

———◆———

Q. Houston-born Meredith MacRae co-starred as Billie Joe in what television series set in the small town of Hooterville?

A. "Petticoat Junction."

———◆———

Q. Where was singer/guitarist Buck Owens born?

A. Sherman.

———◆———

Q. What former Las Vegas showgirl born in Galveston made her screen debut in the 1972 film *Slaughterhouse Five?*

A. Valerie Perrine.

———◆———

Q. San Antonio-born actor Al Freeman, Jr., plays Lieutenant Ed Hall in what daytime soap opera?

A. "One Life to Live."

———◆———

Q. What Lubbock-born musician was known as the "King of the White Texas Bluesmen"?

A. Delbert McClinton.

Q. In what community was a replica of the Alamo constructed for use in filming the 1959 movie *The Alamo*?

A. Brackettville.

◆

Q. Country singer Billie Jo Spears was born in what Texas city?

A. Beaumont.

◆

Q. What Houston-born actress appeared in the television productions of *The Entertainer* and *Stand By Your Man*?

A. Annette O'Toole.

◆

Q. Brownsville-born Bernard Kowalski was executive producer and director of what 1970s crime drama starring Robert Blake?

A. "Baretta."

◆

Q. What singer born in Erath County was a featured performer on the ABC-TV show "Shindig?"

A. Jerry Naylor.

◆

Q. In 1980 what singer born in Palestine had the country music hit "Raisin' Cane in Texas"?

A. Gene Watson.

◆

Q. What Texan gained fame with such movies as *Red Dawn* and *Dirty Dancing*?

A. Patrick Swayze.

HISTORY

C H A P T E R   T H R E E

Q. In 1909 what Dallas store became the first in the state of install escalators?

A. Sanger Brothers.

———◆———

Q. Who busted "Doc" Holliday out of jail in Fort Griffin by setting fire to the building?

A. "Doc's" lady friend Big Nose Kate.

———◆———

Q. What television station became the first in the nation to offer educational programming in 1953?

A. KUHT-TV, Houston.

———◆———

Q. Though the Texas Rangers trace their roots back to 1823, in what year was the agency officially organized?

A. 1835.

———◆———

Q. In 1948 what colorful, self-admitted Memphis bootlegger, with some 65 counts on his police record, ran for sheriff of Hall County?

A. Raymond Ballew.

Q. What Texas governor was founder of the Humble Oil and Refining Company?

A. Ross S. Sterling.

◆

Q. The attempt by Mexican authorities to retrieve what item from the colonists at Gonzales led to the "first shot for Texas independence" being fired?

A. A small brass cannon.

◆

Q. How many naval fliers were trained at the Corpus Christi Naval Air Station during World War II?

A. 40,000.

◆

Q. Where did the Kiowa chief Satana, called the "Orator of the Plains," jump to his death on October 11, 1878?

A. The Huntsville penitentiary.

◆

Q. In 1928 Lyndon B. Johnson taught school in what small south Texas town in order to earn the money to return to college?

A. Cotulla.

◆

Q. Who was the only adult male survivor of the Alamo?

A. A black slave named Joe.

◆

Q. Who was the first native-born governor of Texas?

A. James Stephen ("Jim") Hogg.

Q. What structure standing on the grounds of the Depot Museum in Henderson was the first of its kind to receive a historical marker?

A. "Arnold Outhouse," an ornate 3-holer.

◆

Q. Over what adjoining area did the Republic of Texas attempt to extend its jurisdiction in 1841?

A. New Mexico.

◆

Q. Gunslinger Jim Courtright, who served as marshall in Fort Worth, later opened what protection racket then disguised as a business?

A. Commercial Detective Agency.

◆

Q. What unique voting event took place in Texas for the first time in 1918?

A. Women were allowed to vote.

◆

Q. What honor was bestowed upon Scout Bill Dixon and his four surviving companions following the Battle of Buffalo Wallow in Hemphill County in 1874?

A. The Congressional Medal of Honor.

◆

Q. What famous pirate headquartered on Galveston Island from 1817 to 1821?

A. Jean Lafitte.

◆

Q. Where, in October of 1911, was the first 48-star U.S. flag flown in the nation?

A. Fort Bliss.

Q. Between 1911 and 1914 what cereal king spent some $50,000 on dynamite for rain-making experiments around the town that bears his name?

A. C. W. Post.

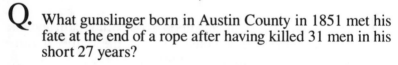

Q. How many troops were trained at Fort Bliss during the Mexican border conflicts of 1916 and 1917?

A. 60,000.

Q. What primitive cannibalistic tribe of Indians inhabited the barrier island along the coast of Texas when the first Europeans arrived?

A. Karankawa Indians.

Q. What was Kit Carson's last military battle?

A. First battle of Adobe Walls, Stinnett.

Q. What gunslinger born in Austin County in 1851 met his fate at the end of a rope after having killed 31 men in his short 27 years?

A. Bill Longley.

Q. George Bush was first elected to what public office in 1966?

A. United States Representative from Texas.

Q. By what popular name was the Southern Overland Mail line called?

A. The Butterfield Stage Line.

Q. What was Richard King's occupation prior to amassing the fabled King Ranch?

A. Steamboat captain on the Rio Grande.

◆

Q. Where on May 8, 1846, was the first battle of the Mexican war fought?

A. Palo Alto.

◆

Q. What San Antonian became the first pilot to give exhibition flights in China and Japan?

A. Katherine Stinson.

◆

Q. Texas politician John Nance Garner was commonly called by what nickname?

A. "Cactus Jack."

◆

Q. The Texas Navy, which existed from 1835 to 1837, consisted of how many vessels?

A. Four schooners.

◆

Q. What 1952 gubernatorial candidate ran on both the Democratic and Republican tickets?

A. Alan Shivers.

◆

Q. What notorious stagecoach and train robber was shot by Texas Rangers at Round Rock on July 19, 1878?

A. Sam Bass.

Q. What Confederate Texas governor fled to Monterrey, Mexico, where he died in July of 1865?

A. Pendleton Murrah.

———◆———

Q. What state-sponsored college opened its doors for the first time in 1883?

A. University of Texas.

———◆———

Q. How many of the 61 signers of the Texas Declaration of Independence were native Texans?

A. Two (Jose Antonio Navarro and Jose Francisco Ruiz).

———◆———

Q. What is the state's largest and oldest state-supported historical museum?

A. Panhandle Plains Historical Museum.

———◆———

Q. In 1928 what company built the first million-barrel oil tank in Texas at Monahans?

A. Shell Oil Company.

———◆———

Q. What now world-renowned store opened in Dallas in 1907?

A. Neiman-Marcus.

———◆———

Q. What graduate of Texas Wesleyan and Texas Tech became president of Panama in 1972?

A. Demetrio ("Jimmy") Lakas.

Q. What gunfighter was gunned down in the Harris Theatre in Austin in 1884, along with Ben Thompson?

A. King Fisher.

◆

Q. What Spanish explorer first mapped the coastline of Texas in 1519?

A. Alonso Alvarez de Pineda.

◆

Q. What was the name of the B-50 Superfortress that began and completed the first non-stop global flight at Carswell Air Force Base in 1949?

A. "Lucky Lady."

◆

Q. Who became the first woman to be licensed as a dentist in Texas in 1894?

A. Mary Lou Shelman.

◆

Q. What nickname was given to the men who captured or killed wild horses on the plains of Texas?

A. "Mustangers."

◆

Q. Who in 1971 became the first Texan appointed Secretary of the Navy?

A. John Connally.

◆

Q. What famous trailblazer from Tennessee was a fatality of the Battle of the Alamo?

A. David ("Davy") Crockett.

Q. In 1885 what now internationally famous soft drink was originated at Morrison's Old Corner Drug Store in Waco?

A. Dr Pepper.

———◆———

Q. In 1925 who became the first woman in Texas, and the second woman in the nation, to serve as governor?

A. Miriam A. Ferguson.

———◆———

Q. Built in 1887, what courthouse is one of the oldest buildings in the state made of handmade slate bricks?

A. Leon County Courthouse.

———◆———

Q. In 1851 what became the first railroad line to lay track in the state?

A. The Buffalo Bayou, Brazos & Colorado Railroad.

———◆———

Q. What settlement became the first colonial capital of Texas?

A. Monclova, Coahuila, Mexico.

———◆———

Q. Who was appointed Commander in Chief of the Army of Texas on October 10, 1835?

A. Stephen F. Austin.

———◆———

Q. How many lives were lost in the March 18, 1937, New London High School gas explosion?

A. 293 (279 students, 12 teachers, and two persons visiting the school).

Q. Under Mexican rule what was the compulsory religious faith imposed on all Texan colonists?

A. Roman Catholic.

—◆—

Q. Who became Dallas's first elected woman mayor?

A. Annette Strauss.

—◆—

Q. Where was the last land battle of the War Between the States fought on May 12–13, 1865?

A. Palmito Hill.

—◆—

Q. Under the terms of its annexation with the United States, Texas may, of its own choosing, divide itself into how many states?

A. Five.

—◆—

Q. What native Texan became the most decorated U.S. soldier of World War II?

A. Audie Murphy.

—◆—

Q. Who was the notorious Reconstruction Period desperado from the Texarkana area?

A. Cullen Baker.

—◆—

Q. Between what two municipalities was the first concrete highway constructed in Texas in 1920?

A. Harlingen and San Benito.

Q. What notorious female outlaw of the 1870s and 1880s lived near Dallas at one time?

A. Belle Starr.

Q. What Cisco museum was the first hotel in the Hilton chain?

A. Mobley Hotel.

Q. What West Texas-born gunfighter and gambler owned an interest in the famous Long Branch Saloon in Dodge City, Kansas, and later owned the White Elephant Saloon in Fort Worth?

A. Luke Short.

Q. Where was Texas billionaire Howard Robard Hughes born in 1905?

A. Houston.

Q. Where was Baylor University founded in 1845?

A. Independence.

Q. What large Texas observatory was dedicated on May 5, 1939?

A. McDonald Observatory near Fort Davis.

Q. What railroad chartered in 1909 by Tim Cronin had switches in Williamson County with such names as Matthew, Mark, Luke and John?

A. The Gospel Railroad.

Q. In 1876, who established the first large Panhandle ranch?

A. Colonel Charles Goodnight.

◆

Q. What was the source of revenue used to finance the construction of the first Hays County courthouse in San Marcos?

A. Two thousand dollars in forfeited bail money.

◆

Q. What municipality became the first in Texas to treat its dirt streets with oil in 1898?

A. Corsicana.

◆

Q. In what city is the Georgia Monument, honoring the Georgia Battalion that fought in Texas' war for independence?

A. Albany.

◆

Q. Who is credited with providing personal funds that prevented the sale and demolition of the Alamo in 1903?

A. Clara Driscoll.

◆

Q. In what Real County community did Charles A. Lindbergh make an unscheduled street landing in 1923 after losing his bearings?

A. Camp Wood.

◆

Q. What Texas governor never held a political office until he was elected to the governorship?

A. Thomas Mitchell Campbell (1907–11).

Q. What was the name of Judge Roy Bean's famous combination courtroom and saloon?

A. The Jersey Lily.

———◆———

Q. Kelly Field was established near San Antonio in 1917 with how many airplanes?

A. Four.

———◆———

Q. In what year did women first serve as jurors in the Texas judicial system?

A. 1954.

———◆———

Q. What Spanish explorer was involved in expeditions to the Rio Grande region in 1520 and 1523?

A. Francisco Garay.

———◆———

Q. On November 9, 1881, what important government building in Austin was destroyed by fire?

A. The State Capitol building.

———◆———

Q. What founder of *The Northern Standard* is considered the "father of Texas journalism"?

A. Col. Charles DeMorse.

———◆———

Q. In what year were the first license plates issued in Texas?

A. 1917.

Q. What gunfighter and one-time marshal of Austin was known for his tall silk hat?

A. Ben Thompson.

Q. Detaining some 6,000 Union troops, what was the largest POW camp in Texas during the War Between the States?

A. Camp Ford at Tyler.

Q. What Texas-born Democrat became the first black woman elected to the United States Congress from a southern state?

A. Barbara C. Jordan.

Q. Where did Stephen F. Austin die of pneumonia in 1836?

A. West Columbia.

Q. On May 25, 1690, what became the first mission established in east Texas?

A. Mission San Francisco de los Tejas.

Q. John Nance Garner served the Franklin D. Roosevelt administration in what capacity?

A. Vice president (1933–41).

Q. On April 6, 1830, the Mexican government placed a ban on immigration into Texas from what country?

A. The United States of America.

Q. Where in 1890 was Major General Claire Lee Chennault, who founded the famous "Flying Tigers," born?

A. Commerce.

———◆———

Q. In what Galveston museum does "the People's Gallery" feature a lifesize re-creation of a busy depot scene of the 1930s?

A. Center for Transportation and Commerce (Railroad Museum).

———◆———

Q. Who was known across the Texas frontier as the "fightin' parson"?

A. Andrew Jackson ("Jack") Potter.

———◆———

Q. On what date was President John F. Kennedy assassinated in Dallas?

A. November 22, 1963.

———◆———

Q. The French founded what fort on Garcitas Creek at Matagorda Bay in 1685?

A. Fort St. Louis.

———◆———

Q. What percentage of Texas's population was rural in 1900?

A. 82 percent.

———◆———

Q. About how many lives were lost in the hurricane and tidal wave that struck Galveston on September 8, 1900?

A. 6,000.

Q. What Wharton sheriff was so widely respected that trains had to be charted to accommodate the crowd at his funeral (1894)?

A. Hamilton B. Dickson.

———◆———

Q. For how many consecutive years did Sam Rayburn serve as a member of the U.S. House of Representatives?

A. 49 years.

———◆———

Q. Where in 1915 was the former President of Mexico, Victoriano Huerta, imprisoned?

A. Fort Bliss.

———◆———

Q. What was the first hospital erected in Temple in 1891?

A. The Gulf, Colorado and Santa Fe Railroad Hospital.

———◆———

Q. What was the chief commercial occupation of the Anglo-American colonists in the pre-Republic era?

A. Cotton farming.

———◆———

Q. Who became the first black in Texas arriving with the Cabeza de Vaca expedition in 1528?

A. Estevanico.

———◆———

Q. In what state was William Barret Travis born?

A. South Carolina.

Q. In 1901 what Baptist minister built and allegedly flew his Bible-inspired "Ezekiel Airship"?

A. Rev. Burrel Cannon.

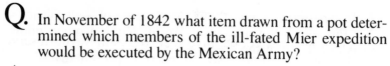

Q. In November of 1842 what item drawn from a pot determined which members of the ill-fated Mier expedition would be executed by the Mexican Army?

A. Black beans.

Q. Unbranded strays of what Texas cattleman gave rise in 1845 to the term *maverick?*

A. Samuel A. Maverick.

Q. What Terrell museum honors the glider pilots of World War II?

A. Silent Wings Museum.

Q. What animals were introduced into Texas in 1856 to provide transportation to Army soldiers?

A. Camels.

Q. Who served as the last president of the Republic of Texas?

A. Anson Jones.

Q. Where were Teddy Roosevelt's famous Rough Riders trained?

A. San Antonio.

Q. Who in 1827 built the first home on the site that eventually became El Paso?

A. Juan Maria Ponce de Leon.

Q. In what county courthouse is a statue of Walt Disney's "Fifinella," the mascot of World War II women pilots who trained in the area?

A. Nolan.

Q. Who drew the first topographical map of Texas in 1835?

A. Gail Borden, Jr.

Q. How many captured Indian horses were ordered killed by General R. S. Mackenzie near the mouth of Tule Creek during his 1874 Panhandle campaign?

A. 1,450.

Q. Founded in 1836, Jefferson grew to what population by 1875?

A. Over 30,000.

Q. Called "the most dangerous man alive" by Wyatt Earp, what gambling gunfighter practiced dentistry in Dallas at one time?

A. Dr. John H. ("Doc") Holliday.

Q. How many Texans served in the military during World War I?

A. Nearly 210,000.

Q. What Tyler resident was the only woman pictured on Confederate money?

A. Lucy Holcombe Pickens.

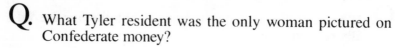

Q. Where did Lyndon B. Johnson receive his oath of office as president of the United States?

A. On board Air Force One at Love Field, Dallas.

Q. For what amount did slaver Luis Aury sell blacks at the Galveston Island slave market in 1816?

A. One dollar a pound.

Q. During what famous three-day Indian battle in 1874 did 28 men and one woman hold off several hundred Comanche, Cheyenne, and Kiowa warriors?

A. The Battle of Adobe Walls.

Q. Opened in 1957, what was the first turnpike in Texas?

A. The Dallas–Fort Worth Turnpike.

Q. In 1928 what airline started the state's first regularly scheduled passenger service?

A. Texas Air Transport.

Q. Where were some 330 Texan prisoners of war massacred by Santa Anna's command on March 27, 1836?

A. Goliad.

Q. When was Texas readmitted as a state following the War Between the States?

A. March 30, 1870.

Q. What was the name of the first radio network established in Texas in 1934?

A. The Texas Quality Network.

Q. Who made the first Texas Lone Star flag?

A. Joanna Troutman (of Georgia).

Q. The Republic of Texas established what government office in 1837 in an attempt to control land fraud and speculator schemes?

A. The General Land Office.

Q. What was the name of the international exposition held in San Antonio in 1968?

A. Hemisfair.

Q. Where in 1923 were the first automatic traffic signals in the nation installed?

A. Dallas.

Q. What two feuding civilian factions created havoc in Shelbyville in the early 1840s?

A. The Regulators and the Moderators.

Q. On July 20, 1969, what word was the first transmitted by a human from the moon?

A. *Houston.*

Q. What Houstonian on December 31, 1944, became the first woman to receive the Distinguished Service Medal?

A. Oveta Culp Hobby.

Q. Begun in 1859 and completed in 1866, what is the oldest courthouse in Texas?

A. Cass County Courthouse, Linden.

Q. What son of an ex-slave became the first black president of a bank in Texas?

A. William Madison ("Gooseneck") McDonald.

Q. What Spearman organization has tried to maintain mule teams and covered wagons for old-fashioned rides across the plains?

A. Rolling Plains Mule Train Association.

Q. In 1874 what special division of Texas Rangers was organized to bring stability to the western part of Texas?

A. The Frontier Battalion.

Q. Constructed in 1928, Randolph Field was given what title?

A. "West Point of the Air."

Q. What Texas governor of the 1870s weighed between 350 and 400 pounds?

A. Richard Bennet Hubbard.

———◆———

Q. In what year did the city of Houston secure deep water passage?

A. 1915.

———◆———

Q. At Fort Sam Houston Lieutenant Benjamin Foulois became the first pilot to utilize what aeronautical innovation in 1910?

A. Landing wheels.

———◆———

Q. The mob execution of Charles H. Howard, John McBride, and John Atkinson at San Elizario ended what 1877 west Texas conflict?

A. The Salt War.

———◆———

Q. What part of the Johnson Space Center became the nerve center for America's manned space program in 1965?

A. The Mission Control Center.

———◆———

Q. What Texas governor is reported to have spent a sum total of only thirty-five cents on his campaign?

A. Oran Milo Roberts (1879–83).

———◆———

Q. Who in 1898 established the Bermuda onion industry in Laredo?

A. Thomas C. Nye.

Q. What amount did Secretary of State Henry Clay offer Mexico in 1825 to cede Texas to the United States?

A. One million dollars.

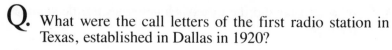

Q. What were the call letters of the first radio station in Texas, established in Dallas in 1920?

A. WRR.

Q. On what date did the Alamo fall to Santa Anna's troops?

A. March 6, 1836.

Q. What Mexican border outlaw captured Brownsville in 1859?

A. Juan Cortinas.

Q. Lyndon B. Johnson received his B.S. degree from what Texas school?

A. Southwest Texas State Teachers College.

Q. In 1921 what Texas city became the first to have all dial telephones?

A. Wichita Falls.

Q. In what community was the first skirmish of the Texas Revolution fought?

A. Gonzales.

Q. What San Antonian served with Neil Armstrong in accomplishing the first U.S. space docking?

A. David R. Scott.

———◆———

Q. Who in 1846 became the first governor of the state of Texas?

A. James Pinckney Henderson.

———◆———

Q. What Dallas billionaire made his initial fortune speculating in Arkansas oil?

A. Haroldson Lafayette Hunt.

———◆———

Q. Who in 1846 were the first two men to represent the state of Texas in the United States Senate?

A. Thomas J. Rusk and Sam Houston.

———◆———

Q. What action was taken by Texas in February of 1861 following a ratification vote by its citizens?

A. Secession from the Union.

———◆———

Q. For what presidential candidate did Texas cast its electoral votes in 1984?

A. President Ronald Reagan.

———◆———

Q. What Dallas night club owner shot and killed alleged presidential assassin Lee Harvey Oswald at Dallas City Jail on November 24, 1963?

A. Jack Ruby.

Q. In 1840 who established a trading post and community that later became the city of Dallas?

A. John Neely Bryan.

———◆———

Q. In operation since 1936, what is the Texas Highway Department's oldest ferry?

A. The Galveston to Port Boliver.

———◆———

Q. What document was adopted on March 2, 1836, at Washington on the Brazos River?

A. The Texas Declaration of Independence.

———◆———

Q. Who in 1966 became the first woman to represent Texas in the U.S. House of Representatives?

A. Mrs. Lera Thomas.

———◆———

Q. The annexation of Texas immediately brought about what international conflict?

A. The Mexican War.

———◆———

Q. In 1967 President Lyndon B. Johnson appointed what Texan to the office of Attorney General?

A. Ramsey Clark.

———◆———

Q. In 1889 Texas became the second state in the nation to enact what type of laws?

A. Anti-trust laws.

Q. At one time the Confederate Capital of the State of Missouri was officially situated in what east Texas town?

A. Marshall.

Q. In 1879 what gambler and saloonkeeper left his entire estate of $15,000 to the Denison public schools?

A. Justin Raynal.

Q. What community is believed to be the oldest Polish settlement in the United States?

A. Panna Maria.

Q. Who on December 21, 1821, at Bolivar Point became the first Anglo-American baby to be born in Texas?

A. Mary James Long.

Q. What three major oil companies can trace their roots to the Spindletop oil boom?

A. Gulf, Texaco, and Mobil.

Q. Who was the Natchez, Mississippi, resident who led two expeditions into Texas from 1819 to 1821 in an attempt to secure its independence?

A. Dr. James Long.

Q. In 1978 what Republican governor was elected, the first since 1869?

A. William P. Clements.

Q. In 1895 what eccentric millionaire established Port Arthur based on directions he said came to him from supernatural creatures of the spirit world?

A. Arthur Edward Stilwell.

Q. In 1872 what railroad line entered Texas at Denison?

A. The Missouri, Kansas and Texas.

Q. What Pasadena attraction includes a working turn-of-the-century farm?

A. Armand Bayou Nature Center.

Q. What workers' strike on April 30, 1934, brought unrest to Houston?

A. The Longshoremen's Strike.

Q. On May 17, 1835, what para-military organization was formed at Bastrop on the Colorado River?

A. The Committee of Safety.

Q. Where in 1906 did black soldiers of the 25th Infantry riot?

A. Brownsville.

Q. What base at Wichita Falls served as a principle training field for Army Air Corp recruits during World War II?

A. Sheppard Field, Sheppard Air Force Base.

Q. Who formally founded Villa de Laredo on May 15, 1755?

A. Tómas Sánchez.

---◆---

Q. What Glen Rose resident of the 1870s made a deathbed claim to his lawyer that he was John Wilkes Booth?

A. John St. Helen.

---◆---

Q. How many family members and servants of the defenders survived the battle at the Alamo?

A. Sixteen.

---◆---

Q. How many Fort Worth blocks were destroyed by the devastating fire of 1909?

A. Twenty.

---◆---

Q. In 1958 billionaire H. L. Hunt established what radio program on which he could voice his political views?

A. "Life Line."

---◆---

Q. In one of railroad's greatest track laying races, what line beat Jay Gould's Texas and Pacific Railroad into El Paso on May 19, 1881?

A. Southern Pacific Railroad.

---◆---

Q. What Texas governor was deposed from office for refusing to support the Confederacy?

A. Sam Houston.

Q. Born near Grand Saline, what pioneer high-altitude pilot became the first person to fly solo around the world in 1933?

A. Wiley Hardeman Post.

Q. How many fighting men attempted to defend the Alamo against Santa Anna's 5,000 Mexican soldiers in 1836?

A. Between 185 and 200.

Q. What "mass transit" system was inaugurated in Dallas in 1873?

A. Mule-drawn streetcars.

Q. In what town is there a replica of the Ezekiel Airship, built following a description in the Bible?

A. Pittsburg.

Q. What group of east Texas Indians were culturally similar to the Mound Builders of the Mississippi Valley?

A. Caddo.

Q. In 1826 what disgruntled Anglo-American colonist organized a short-lived rebellion in Texas and declared it the Republic of Fredonia?

A. Hayden Edwards.

Q. Who was selected majority leader of the U.S. House of Representatives in 1976?

A. James Claude Wright, Jr.

Q. Between what two towns in 1907 was the first bus service in Texas established?

A. Colorado City and Snyder.

———◆———

Q. What famous frontier scout, along with 396 Federal troops, engaged some 1,000 Indian warriors in an all-day battle near Adobe Walls in 1864?

A. Colonel Kit Carson.

———◆———

Q. By what treaty with Spain did the United States formally relinquish all claims to Texas?

A. The Treaty of 1819.

———◆———

Q. Where was the first Women's Christian Temperance Union established in Texas in 1882?

A. Paris.

———◆———

Q. What education-related law was enacted in Texas in 1915?

A. The Compulsory Attendance Law.

———◆———

Q. What name did the Cherokee Indians give to Sam Houston?

A. *Co-lon-neh* ("the Raven").

———◆———

Q. What two men were the leaders of forces that invaded Texas and captured San Antonio in 1813?

A. Bernardo Gutierrez and Augustus W. Magee.

Q. Under Mexican rule Anglo-American colonists were denied what major legal right?

A. Trial by jury.

———◆———

Q. In what year did the Texas legislature enact a law prohibiting malicious fence cutting in reaction to the Fence-cutting War?

A. 1884.

———◆———

Q. What unique Dallas businesswoman built the first iron bridge across the Trinity River?

A. Sarah Cockrell.

———◆———

Q. What organization led in aiding freed slaves in relocation, education, and vocational opportunities following the War Between the States?

A. Freedmen's Bureau.

———◆———

Q. What ethnic group first settled in Texas at Castroville in 1844?

A. Alsatians.

———◆———

Q. How many Anglo-American colonists did Stephen F. Austin bring into Texas between 1821 and 1831?

A. Approximately 5,600.

———◆———

Q. What city is the birthplace of the first and second native-born Texans to serve as governor?

A. Rusk.

Q. In 1854 Sam Houston was converted, baptized, and became a member of what historic Texas church?

A. Independence Baptist Church at Independence.

———◆———

Q. What railroad company established Texarkana in 1873?

A. The Texas and Pacific Railway.

———◆———

Q. Where was the first municipal high school in Texas established in 1875?

A. Brenham.

———◆———

Q. At what two settlements did battles occur between Texas farmers and Mexican soldiers in June of 1832?

A. Anahuac and Velasco.

———◆———

Q. What was the total assessed value of slaves in Texas in 1860?

A. $64,000,000.

———◆———

Q. In 1876 what educational facility became the first state-sponsored college in Texas?

A. Agricultural and Mechanical College of Texas.

———◆———

Q. Established in 1681, what is the oldest mission in Texas?

A. Corpus Christi de la Isleta, El Paso.

Q. What county courthouse was built in 1884–86 at a cost of $55,555.55?

A. Parker.

Q. By what titles were private schools in Texas called during the 1820s and 1830s?

A. "Cornfield" or "old fields" schools.

Q. What entity was established in 1919 to oversee state fiscal and budget policies?

A. State Board of Control.

Q. Approximately how many Texans enlisted in the Union army during the War Between the States?

A. 2,000.

Q. What steam-powered river freighter was built and launched at Dallas in 1868?

A. The *Sallie Haynes*.

Q. What Republic of Texas president pressed for the establishment of a public school system?

A. Mirabeau B. Lamar.

Q. Where was a provisional Texas government adopted on November 3, 1835?

A. San Felipe.

Q. Who, on behalf of the Federal government, declared the freedom of all slaves and the nullification of Confederate laws at Galveston on June 19, 1865?

A. General Gordon Granger.

---◆---

Q. Under whose leadership did Texans lay siege to San Antonio on October 28, 1835?

A. James Bowie and James W. Fannin, Jr.

---◆---

Q. What new type of fencing material was introduced into Texas in the mid-1870s?

A. Barbed wire.

---◆---

Q. What Galveston newspaper publisher had the state's first telephones installed in 1878?

A. Col. A. H. Belo.

---◆---

Q. How long was Stephen F. Austin imprisoned in Mexico for presenting a Texas state constitution to Mexican authorities in 1833?

A. Almost two years and three months.

---◆---

Q. What other two names were applied to Texas by early explorers?

A. Amichel and New Philippines.

---◆---

Q. What town became the first in the state to purchase a motorized fire engine in 1909?

A. Big Spring.

Q. Where was Texas civil government headquartered when Texas was a Spanish province?

A. San Antonio de Bexar.

———◆———

Q. In 1828 what educational aid was provided free of charge for the first time in Texas at a public school in San Antonio?

A. Textbooks.

———◆———

Q. Who was the first sheriff of Navarro County?

A. James Buckner ("Buck") Barry.

———◆———

Q. What type of postal service was inaugurated between San Antonio and San Diego on August 9, 1857?

A. Overland mail coach service.

———◆———

Q. What rail line was called the "Boll Weevil Line" during the early twentieth century?

A. Trinity and Brazos Valley Railway.

———◆———

Q. What Texan became the first United States Secretary of Health, Education, and Welfare?

A. Oveta Culp Hobby.

———◆———

Q. Who in the 1928 election became the first Republican presidential candidate to carry the state of Texas?

A. Herbert Hoover.

ARTS & LITERATURE

Q. Fort Worth native Roger Miller composed the music for what Broadway play?

A. *Big River*.

———◆———

Q. What El Paso-born journalist became a White House correspondent in 1977?

A. Sam Donaldson.

———◆———

Q. Where was black composer Scott Joplin, the "King of Ragtime," born in 1868?

A. Texarkana.

———◆———

Q. Who painted the *Surrender of Santa Anna?*

A. William Henry Huddle.

———◆———

Q. In what city is Robert Glen's *The Mustangs of Las Colinas*, a lifesize sculpture of nine horses?

A. Irving.

Q. Where was world-famous prima donna Yvonne de Treville born?

A. Galveston.

———◆———

Q. The American Institute of Architects placed what Galveston landmark on its list of the nation's 100 outstanding buildings?

A. Bishop's Palace.

———◆———

Q. What Fredericksburg pageant retells the legend of a pioneer woman calming her children's fears during uncertain times?

A. *Easter Fires*.

———◆———

Q. Who is the most widely read of Texas poets?

A. Grace Noll Crowell.

———◆———

Q. Due to a lack of newsprint, what type of paper did the *Victoria Advocate* use during the War Between the States?

A. Wallpaper and butcher paper.

———◆———

Q. Who was considered the "grand old man" of Texas sculpture?

A. Frank Teich.

———◆———

Q. What mid-nineteenth century novelist produced such Texas based works as *The Rifle Rangers*, *The Scalp Hunters*, and *The Headless Horseman?*

A. Mayne Reid.

Q. What University of Texas professor/writer was a leading authority on Texas tales and folklore?

A. James Frank Dobie.

◆

Q. The Houston Museum of Fine Arts displays Italian and Spanish High Renaissance art from what collection?

A. The Kress Collection.

◆

Q. What Dallas building houses a 124-by-20-foot painting depicting the biblical miracle at Pentecost?

A. Biblical Arts Center.

◆

Q. For what craft was pioneer era artisan Samuel Bell of San Antonio best known?

A. Silversmithing.

◆

Q. The Lyndon Baines Johnson Library is on what college campus?

A. The University of Texas at Austin.

◆

Q. Who originated the *Texas Almanac* in 1857?

A. Willard Richardson.

◆

Q. What was the name of mythical folk hero Pecos Bill's horse?

A. Widow Maker.

Q. Displayed at the Dallas Museum of Art, *Stake Hitch* is a giant-scale sculpture designed and crafted by what artist?

A. Claes Oldenburg.

———◆———

Q. In what Texas library is the world's largest collection of material about and by poet Robert Browning?

A. The Armstrong Browning Library, Baylor University.

———◆———

Q. Peaster native Robert E. Howard who created numerous adventure books was best known for what character?

A. Conan the Barbarian.

———◆———

Q. What distinguished composer and conductor was born at Fredericksburg in 1858?

A. Frank van der Stucken.

———◆———

Q. Who was the director of the Dallas Little Theater from 1923 to 1931?

A. Oliver Hinsdale.

———◆———

Q. Larry McMurtry's 1961 novel, *Horseman, Pass By,* became the basis for what motion picture?

A. *Hud.*

———◆———

Q. What world famous sculptor was commissioned to do the Ballinger *Cowboy and His Horse* statue, honoring Charles H. Noyes?

A. Pompeo Coppini.

Q. Established in 1853, what is the oldest weekly newspaper in Texas?

A. *The Bastrop Advertiser*.

Q. What subject matter became the hallmark of Merkel-born etcher James Swann?

A. Trees.

Q. What Waco native was first to publicly sing "Old Man River" in the 1927 presentation of *Showboat?*

A. Jules Bledsoe.

Q. Cotton and Blackie Scantling are the main characters in what 1949 Texas-based work by Fred Gipson?

A. *Hound-Dog Man*.

Q. What German immigrant ushered in the era of modern sculpture in Texas?

A. Elisabet Ney.

Q. By whom were the historical paintings *Dawn at the Alamo* and *Battle of San Jacinto* created?

A. H. S. McArdle.

Q. The comprehensive collection of American Folk Songs of the Library of Congress is largely due to the dedication of what Austin native?

A. Alan Lomax.

Q. From whose artwork were the first postcards with blue-bonnet scenes created?

A. Ethel Dixon.

———◆———

Q. What Galveston landmark is the only building in Texas on the American Institute of Architects' list of 100 out-standing buildings?

A. Bishop's Palace.

———◆———

Q. Where is the famous *Diamond Bessie Murder Trial* play performed?

A. The old Jewish Synagogue, Jefferson.

———◆———

Q. What University of Dallas professor started GLA Press?

A. June Welch.

———◆———

Q. Artist Richard Lippold sculpted what work that graces the lobby of the Jesse H. Jones Hall for Performing Arts in Houston?

A. *Gemini II.*

———◆———

Q. What was the name of the first Dallas newspaper, founded in 1849?

A. *The Cedar Snag.*

———◆———

Q. In 1971 what native Dallas painter became the first per-son to be designated the official state artist by the Texas legislature?

A. Joe Ruiz Grandee.

Q. *The Raven,* written by Marquis James in 1929, is a biographical work on what Texas hero?

A. Sam Houston.

Q. Where was the first newspaper in Texas published in 1813?

A. Nacogdoches.

Q. Larry L. King, who wrote . . . *and Other Dirty Stories* and *The One-Eyed Man,* was born in what west Texas town?

A. Putnam.

Q. In 1929 what composition became the official Texas state song?

A. "Texas Our Texas."

Q. Paul Horgan authored what Pulitzer Prize-winning work that became the basis for a symphony?

A. *Great River: The Rio Grande in North American History.*

Q. World famous artist Pompeo Coppini crafted what sculpture that adorns the lawn of the Ballinger courthouse?

A. *The Cowboy and His Horse.*

Q. What Houston-born actress created the column "Texas Gal in Hollywood" from 1952 through 1954?

A. Olive Kathryn Grandstaff (Kathryn Crosby).

Q. What historic home is on the grounds of the Dallas Arboretum and Botanical Gardens?

A. DeGolyer House.

◆

Q. What early Texas portrait painter is best known for her rendering of Mrs. Sam Houston?

A. Penelope Thomas Crouch.

◆

Q. Recreation, sports, and Boy Scouting are subjects of what juvenile magazine published at Irving?

A. *Boy's Life*.

◆

Q. What Dallas drama patron pioneered theater-in-the-round?

A. Margo Jones.

◆

Q. Under what pen name did William Sidney Porter write?

A. O. Henry.

◆

Q. What company became the first publisher of music in Texas in 1866?

A. Thomas Goggan Publishing.

◆

Q. What art organization was founded in San Antonio in March of 1949?

A. The Texas Watercolor Society.

Q. Architect E. E. Myers of Detroit, Michigan, designed what Austin building that was dedicated in 1888?

A. The Texas state capitol.

———◆———

Q. What 1819 novel published in Paris, France, is believed to be the first ever written with a Texas setting?

A. *L'Heroine du Texas.*

———◆———

Q. What facility is home for the Corpus Christi Symphony?

A. Bayfront Plaza Auditorium.

———◆———

Q. The four sculptures entitled *Backs* adorning Burnett Park in Fort Worth were created by what famous French artist?

A. Henri Matisse.

———◆———

Q. The Texas Woodcarvers Rally is hosted by what community?

A. Glen Rose.

———◆———

Q. What writer from Bosque County published his classic work *Adventures of a Ballad Hunter* in 1947?

A. John A. Lomax.

———◆———

Q. Texas painter Alexander Hogue produced what 1936 work that was purchased by the French government?

A. *Drouth Survivors.*

Q. Texas artist Mary Bonner was noted for what art form?

A. Etchings.

---◆---

Q. In what work did *Dallas Morning News* cartoonist Jack Patton and writer John Rosenfield bring state history to life?

A. *Texas History Movies*.

---◆---

Q. What was the name of William Sidney Porter's humorous weekly magazine published in Austin?

A. *The Rolling Stone*.

---◆---

Q. What organization was formed in Lubbock in 1951 to nurture art in the Panhandle area of Texas?

A. The South Plains Art Guild.

---◆---

Q. In 1939 what J. Frank Dobie book received the first award given by the Texas Institute of Letters?

A. *Apache Gold and Yaqui Silver*.

---◆---

Q. The region of east Dickens County is described in what Zane Grey tale?

A. *The Thundering Herd*.

---◆---

Q. A replica of the U.S. Capitol office of Sam Rayburn is contained in what Texas building?

A. The Sam Rayburn Library, Bonham.

Q. What is the title of Bob Wills' biography written by Charles R. Townsend?

A. *San Antonio Rose.*

───────◆───────

Q. College Station features what spring musical event?

A. The Annual Jazz Festival.

───────◆───────

Q. What Denton landmark has been called "the most picturesque pile of rocks in North Texas"?

A. Denton County Courthouse.

───────◆───────

Q. The Dallas Theater Center was designed by what noted architect?

A. Frank Lloyd Wright.

───────◆───────

Q. What title did American stage director Joshua Logan give to his first autobiography?

A. *Josh, My Up and Down, In and Out Life.*

───────◆───────

Q. Marjorie Merriwether Post, daughter of cereal King C. W. Post, donated a collection of Old Masters art to what Texas facility?

A. South Plains College Art Museum.

───────◆───────

Q. Who produced the unique work *On the Trail of Negro Folksongs* in 1925?

A. Dorothy Scarborough.

Q. Fort Worth hosts what internationally acclaimed piano contest?

A. The Van Cliburn Quadrennial International Piano Competition.

———◆———

Q. What was the name of Texas' first newspaper, published in Nacogdoches?

A. *Gaceta de Tejas*.

———◆———

Q. What town is the home of the Texas Baroque Ensemble?

A. Garland.

———◆———

Q. Who founded the Curtain Club, a drama organization at the University of Texas, in 1909?

A. Stark Young.

———◆———

Q. What newspaper of great importance to the Texas revolution and the Republic was established in San Felipe in 1835?

A. *Telegraph and Texas Register.*

———◆———

Q. By the 1930s what illustrator had become known as the "Dean of Texas Cartoonists"?

A. W. K. Patrick.

———◆———

Q. Who wrote the 1885 work *The Adventure of Big-Foot Wallace, The Texas Ranger and Hunter?*

A. John C. Duval.

Q. What Dallas native painted the official illustration used on 20-Mule Team Borax boxes?

A. Joe Ruiz Grandee.

◆

Q. Who is considered Texas's most distinguished poet?

A. Mrs. Karle Wilson Baker.

◆

Q. The autobiography of actress Evelyn Keyes was published in 1977 under what title?

A. *Scarlett O'Hara's Younger Sister*.

◆

Q. What symphony orchestra in 1933 became the first to feature the work of Texas composers?

A. The Houston Symphony.

◆

Q. In what way did writer O. Henry once refer to the Texas hill country?

A. Austin's violet crown.

◆

Q. What German immigrant brought the first piano into Texas in 1834?

A. Robert Kieberg, Sr.

◆

Q. Where was Texas newspaper journalist Stanley Walker born?

A. Lampasas.

Q. A Gutenburg Bible printed in 1455 is displayed at what Texas museum?

A. The Harry Ransom Center on the campus of the University of Texas, Austin.

———◆———

Q. What work by pioneer Texas painter Edward Grenet was accepted by the Paris Salon?

A. *Romana*.

———◆———

Q. Between 1926 and 1929 what noted Scottish portrait painter taught in Lubbock?

A. Alexander Watson Mack.

———◆———

Q. Maintaining the heritage of early Texas music, what event is held each spring in Llano?

A. Llano Old Time Fiddlers Festival.

———◆———

Q. What 1935 book by Walter Prescott Webb was successfully adapted as a screen play?

A. *The Texas Rangers*.

———◆———

Q. The Rosenberg Library, the first free public library in Texas, is in what city?

A. Galveston.

———◆———

Q. In what year was the Texas Fine Arts Association organized?

A. 1911.

Q. What was the title of Lon Tinkle's 1958 book that used the siege of the Alamo as its setting?

A. *13 Days to Glory.*

———◆———

Q. What was the first nonsectarian university established in the Republic of Texas?

A. Old Nacogdoches University.

———◆———

Q. What artist born in San Antonio in 1882 became the state's most famous painter of bluebonnets?

A. Julian Onderdonk.

———◆———

Q. Who founded the Institute For the Arts at Rice University in 1969?

A. John and Dominique de Menil.

———◆———

Q. What El Paso muralist produced work for the Post Office Department Building in Washington, D.C.?

A. Tom Lea.

———◆———

Q. Who donated the facilities for the first city-owned public library in Dallas in 1901?

A. Andrew Carnegie.

———◆———

Q. What 1925 novel by Dorothy Scarborough dealt with the problems of ranching during the Great Drought of 1885?

A. *The Wind.*

Q. Great Texas feuds are documented in what 1951 book by C. L. Sonnichsen?

A. *I'll Die Before I'll Run.*

Q. The *Dallas News* was established in 1885 by the management of what noted pioneer newspaper?

A. *The Galveston News.*

Q. What was the real name of noted San Antonio-born concert pianist Olga Samaroff?

A. Lucy Hickenlooper.

Q. What Maverick County-born artist is known for his horse soldier illustrations?

A. Randy Steffen.

Q. Who carved the window of the sacristy at Mission San José?

A. Pedro Huizar.

Q. What town was the birthplace of both Baylor University and Mary Hardin-Baylor College?

A. Independence.

Q. What Texas violinist served as the concertmaster of the Metropolitan Opera in New York?

A. Carl Venth.

Q. In 1955 what long-time women's editor for *The Fort Worth Press* published her first book, *All the Women of the Bible?*

A. Edith Dean.

———◆———

Q. Scott Joplin wrote what musical composition based on a publicity stunt at Crush in McLennan County where two locomotives crashed head-on into each other on September 15, 1896?

A. *The Crash at Crush.*

———◆———

Q. In what city is a museum honoring contributions Czechs have made to Texas?

A. Temple (Czech Heritage Museum).

———◆———

Q. Who authored *Belle Starr* in 1941?

A. Burton Rascoe.

———◆———

Q. The largest theological library in the United States is housed in what Texas facility?

A. The Fleming Library, Southwestern Baptist Theological Seminary, Fort Worth.

———◆———

Q. Where was the Texas Boys Choir formed in 1946?

A. Fort Worth.

———◆———

Q. What Houston artist created the decorative sculpture displayed on the San Jacinto Battlefield Monument?

A. William M. McVey.

Q. Who was selected as the first Poet Laureate of Texas in 1932?

A. Judd Mortimer Lewis.

———◆———

Q. What Texas painter who first settled in the Terrell area in 1876 became known for his Longhorn paintings?

A. Frank Reaugh.

———◆———

Q. The Munger family of Amarillo provide the characters for what 1958 novel by Al Dewlen?

A. *The Bone Pickers.*

———◆———

Q. What Texas humorist wrote *Life, and Other Ways to Kill Time*?

A. Mike Nichols.

———◆———

Q. *This Favored Place: The Texas Hill Country* was written by what Kerrville resident?

A. Elroy Bode.

———◆———

Q. What outdoor drama presented in Galveston Island State Park depicts Texas's struggle for independence?

A. *The Lone Star.*

———◆———

Q. What Austin resident wrote *Texas: An Album of History*?

A. James L. Haley.

Q. A degree in jazz music was first offered in 1947 by what Texas university?

A. North Texas State.

———————◆———————

Q. What 1968 work by Shelby Hearon gives an interesting exposé of modern suburban Texas lifestyle?

A. *Armadillo in the Grass*.

———————◆———————

Q. Founded in 1892, what was the first black newspaper in Texas?

A. *Falls County Freeman*.

———————◆———————

Q. What one-time pastor of the First Congregational Church in Dallas compiled the internationally famous work *The Scofield Reference Bible?*

A. Cyrus Ingerson Scofield.

———————◆———————

Q. The Audie Murphy Room is in what library?

A. Walworth Harrison Library, Greenville.

———————◆———————

Q. In 1958 what internationally famous concert pianist from Kilgore became the first musician to be honored with a New York ticker-tape parade?

A. Harvey Lavon ("Van") Cliburn.

———————◆———————

Q. In what municipality was the first theater opened in Texas on June 11, 1838?

A. Houston.

Q. What movie critic wrote the fictional "autobiography," *A Guide to Western Civilization, or My Story*?

A. Joe Bob Briggs (aka John Bloom).

◆

Q. In what production do Albany citizens portray the events of early military and pioneer days?

A. *Fort Griffin Fandangle*.

◆

Q. Who composed "The Eyes of Texas Are Upon You" in 1903?

A. John Long Sinclair.

◆

Q. The nation's largest religious painting, measuring 124 feet in length and 20 feet in height, was created by what Dallas artist?

A. Torger Thompson.

◆

Q. Actress Ann Miller's autobiography was published in 1974 with what title?

A. *Miller's High Life*.

◆

Q. What artist created the comic strip character Alley Oop while living in Iran?

A. V. T. Hamlin.

◆

Q. Thomas Marshall, Addison Clark, and Randolph Clark established what music school at Thorp Spring in 1873?

A. The Add-Ran College.

Q. What Goliad County native became Texas's most distinguished black folklorist?

A. Dr. J. Mason Brewer.

---◆---

Q. In what museum is the only complete set of Steuben Glass, "The United States in Crystal," displayed?

A. The Stark Museum of Art (in Orange).

---◆---

Q. Who is known as the Thoreau of Texas literature?

A. Roy Bedichek.

---◆---

Q. John E. Weems's *A Weekend in September* chronicles what natural disaster?

A. The Galveston hurricane of 1900.

---◆---

Q. What 1952, 1,731-page novel by Madison Cooper was said to be the longest novel ever published in the United States?

A. *Sironia, Texas.*

---◆---

Q. In 1932 what unique orchestra was formed in Houston by Czech musician and director J. Drozda?

A. A tamburash orchestra.

---◆---

Q. What 1903 fictional work by Andy Adams is considered to be a classic on cows and cowboys?

A. *The Log of a Cowboy.*

Q. Where was the first location of the Texas Artist Colony when founded in 1920 by Mollie L. Crowther?

A. Christoval.

———◆———

Q. What Texas native authored the 1980 book *Of Outlaws, Con Men, Whores, Politicians and Other Artists?*

A. Larry L. King.

———◆———

Q. For what 1976 composition did Larry Gatlin receive a Grammy award?

A. "Broken Lady."

———◆———

Q. What internationally known religious recording and book publisher is headquartered in Irving?

A. Word, Inc.

———◆———

Q. *Camp of the Lipanes* and *Comanche Chief* are the two best known works of what mid-nineteenth century Texas painter?

A. Theodore Gentilz.

———◆———

Q. Who wrote the highly successful 1886 book *A Texas Cowboy, or Fifteen Years on the Hurricane Deck of a Spanish Pony?*

A. Charles A. Siringo.

———◆———

Q. What popular novelist with more than sixty books to her credit lived in Texas from 1854 to 1869?

A. Amelia E. Barr.

Q. What was the name of the first newspaper published in Texas?

A. *El Mejicano.*

———◆———

Q. What museum is home to Georgia O'Keefe's *Light Coming on the Plains II*?

A. Amon Carter Museum of Western Art.

———◆———

Q. What Dallas cartoonist created the *Restless Age* comic strip in the 1920s?

A. Jack I. Patton.

———◆———

Q. What Texas art museum houses a portrait of George Washington by Gilbert Stuart?

A. El Paso Museum of Art.

———◆———

Q. What nineteenth-century author was the first Texan to succeed at writing as a full-time occupation?

A. Mollie E. Moore Davis.

———◆———

Q. In what town is the Gem of the Hills Arts and Crafts show held?

A. Blanco.

———◆———

Q. Who established the *Northern Standard* newspaper at Clarksville in 1842?

A. Colonel Charles DeMorse.

Q. What college campus is noted for its authentic replica of the Shakespearean Globe Theater.

A. Odessa Community College.

———◆———

Q. The Columbus monument in Puerto Rico was produced by what San Antonio-born sculptor?

A. Bonnie MacCleary.

———◆———

Q. What Robertson County community was the childhood home of novelist Jewel Gibson?

A. Bald Prairie.

———◆———

Q. Martin Dies authored what book about Communists in the United States?

A. *The Trojan Horse in America.*

———◆———

Q. What collector's 100-acre Eden contains the sculptures of such artists as Alice Aycock, Anthony Caro, and Beverly Pepper?

A. Sue Rowan Pittman.

———◆———

Q. What newspaper founded in 1881 became the first daily in Texas to refuse to print whiskey ads?

A. *Abilene Reporter News.*

———◆———

Q. Who authored the 1905 work *From Cattle Range to Cotton Ranch?*

A. Don Hampton Biggers.

SPORTS & LEISURE

C H A P T E R   F I V E

Q. Who became the first full-time football coach at Rice University?

A. John W. Heisman (1924–28).

＋

Q. Who was the first Texan inducted into the Baseball Hall of Fame at Cooperstown?

A. Tris Speaker.

＋

Q. What Texas theme park was the first in the nation to combine entertainment and a historical theme?

A. Six Flags Over Texas, Arlington.

＋

Q. In 1979 who became the first NCAA tennis singles champ from the University of Texas since Berkeley Bell received the honor in 1929?

A. Kevin Curren.

＋

Q. What Dallas native became the first golfer ever to win the U.S., Canadian, and British Opens all in one year?

A. Lee Trevino.

Q. By what name is the University of Texas Longhorn mascot known?

A. Bevo.

◆

Q. Texas-born Frank Robinson was elected to the National Baseball Hall of Fame in what year?

A. 1982.

◆

Q. What event brings more than 12,000 bicyclists to Wichita Falls every August?

A. The Hotter 'n Hell Bicycle Race.

◆

Q. TCU quarterback Sammy Baugh was affiliated with what NFL team from 1937 to 1952?

A. Washington Redskins.

◆

Q. For what two ball clubs did Bibb Falk play during his 12-year American League career?

A. Chicago White Sox and Cleveland Indians.

◆

Q. In what Olympics did David Greig Browning, Jr., win a gold medal in diving?

A. The 1952 Summer Olympics in Helsinki, Finland.

◆

Q. Where do the Texas Rangers play their home games?

A. Arlington Stadium.

Q. What Houston resident was the first Texan to win a Gold Medal in Olympic boxing in 1968?

A. George Foreman.

———◆———

Q. Major league third baseman Pinky Higgins was a native of what Texas community?

A. Red Oak.

———◆———

Q. What Fort Worth resident held the title of World Champion Trick Roper from 1916 through 1933?

A. Chester ("Chet") Byers.

———◆———

Q. Texas Tech is known by what nickname?

A. Red Raiders.

———◆———

Q. The Dallas Cowboys scored their first NFL victory in 1961 over what team?

A. Pittsburgh Steelers (27–24).

———◆———

Q. In 1977 who became the first Heisman Trophy recipient from the University of Texas at Austin?

A. Earl Campbell.

———◆———

Q. College Station is the location of what multi-million-dollar racing facility?

A. Texas World Speedway.

Q. While playing for the Texas Rangers in 1979, who was the only player in American League history to get 200 or more hits in a season without batting .300?

A. Buddy Bell.

◆

Q. What city's chamber of commerce has a 250-member "Chuck Wagon Gang" that travels the country serving barbeque and promoting the city?

A. Odessa.

◆

Q. Jim Hall of Midland revolutionized automobile racing with what car by utilizing adjustable air foils and an automatic transmission?

A. Chaparral II.

◆

Q. What Texas woman has earned three Olympic medals?

A. Babe Didrikson Zaharias.

◆

Q. Brownsville hosts what colorful four-day annual event with costumes and parades, usually in late February?

A. Charro Days.

◆

Q. In what Texas city was Curt Flood born?

A. Houston.

◆

Q. Who are the only players in the history of the University of Houston basketball to have started every game during their careers?

A. Elvin Hayes and Don Chaney.

Q. What Texan was the first four-time winner of the Indy 500 race?

A. A. J. Foyt.

———◆———

Q. Who was the first Texas native to play in the major leagues?

A. Frank J. Hoffman ("The Texas Wonder").

———◆———

Q. What East Texas festival features the FireAnt Calling Contest and the Rubber Chicken Chunking Contest?

A. The FireAnt Festival and Marketfest, Marshall.

———◆———

Q. Longhorn center Gene Chilton was a 1986 third-round draft choice of what NFL team?

A. St. Louis Cardinals.

———◆———

Q. Where is *Chilympiad,* the Texas official state champion chili cookoff, held each September?

A. San Marcos.

———◆———

Q. What TCU all-star end became the first Southwest Conference player to be recognized by the eastern press as a football all-American?

A. Raymond ("Rags") Matthews, 1926–27.

———◆———

Q. What was the original name of the Houston Astros when they began as a National League expansion franchise in 1962?

A. The Colt 45s.

Q. The University of Texas Longhorns baseball team took the 1983 National Championship by defeating what team?

A. Alabama.

◆

Q. Groesbeck presents what fun-filled, three-day variety event in January?

A. Red Stocking Follies.

◆

Q. What Texas museum has the most complete flying collection of U.S. and foreign World War II combat aircraft?

A. Confederate Air Force Flying Museum, Harlingen.

◆

Q. Placekicker Mike Clendenen of the University of Houston signed to play with what NFL team?

A. Denver Broncos.

◆

Q. What Texan led the American League in hitting in 1961 with a .361 batting average?

A. Norm Cash (with the Detroit Tigers).

◆

Q. The *Dallas Times Herald* named what SMU tackle Defensive Player of the Year in 1985?

A. Jerry Ball.

◆

Q. What town hosts the "Hoop D Do," a three-man street basketball tournament, each fall?

A. Wichita Falls.

Q. What former Texas Tech basketball star set the school record for best free throw percentage in a season with 86.9 percent accuracy?

A. Gerald Myers.

———◆———

Q. Who was chosen Rodeo Queen of the 1950 Houston Fat Stock Show?

A. Olive Kathryn Grandstaff (Kathryn Crosby).

———◆———

Q. In what Dallas hotel did Ty Cobb and Ping Bodie come to blows, climaxing an ongoing feud of many years?

A. The Oriental Hotel.

———◆———

Q. Refugio hosts what statewide sporting event in July?

A. The State Championship Frog Jumping Contest.

———◆———

Q. What Rockwall resident set a world speed record on the Brazos River in a supercharged, alcohol-burning hydroplane in May of 1982?

A. Gary Kehrer (184 m.p.h.).

———◆———

Q. Warren-born outfielder Roy Weatherly played for what clubs during his major league career?

A. Cleveland Indians, New York Yankees, and New York Giants.

———◆———

Q. Who was the first Dallas Cowboy named to the Pro Football Hall of Fame?

A. Bob Lilly.

Q. What train, featuring restored cars from the 1930s-1950s, runs from Houston to Galveston Island?

A. The Texas Limited.

———◆———

Q. *Sporting News* magazine named what Bonham-born second baseman National League Rookie of the Year in 1965?

A. Joe Morgan.

———◆———

Q. What Texas school became world famous for its precision drill and dance team formed in 1940?

A. Kilgore College.

———◆———

Q. What Beaumont-born sports executive and former Houston mayor was instrumental in bringing the National League to Houston in 1962?

A. Roy Hofheinz.

———◆———

Q. What University of Houston track runner set the world record for the 50-yard dash in 1982?

A. Stanley Floyd (5.22 seconds).

———◆———

Q. Waterworld in Houston features what 80-foot, free-fall slide attraction?

A. The Edge.

———◆———

Q. Brownwood is host to what running event?

A. The Bluebonnet Relays.

Q. Curt Flood first signed to play baseball with what major league club?

A. Cincinnati Reds.

———◆———

Q. In what city is the Sun Bowl held?
A. El Paso.

———◆———

Q. Associated Press and United Press International named what basketball coach the 1986 Southwest Conference "Coach of the Year"?

A. Jim Killingsworth, Texas Christian.

———◆———

Q. What Beaumont-born sportswoman was the top money-winner in the first four years of the LPGA tour?

A. Babe Didrikson Zaharias.

———◆———

Q. From 1950 to 1955 Tom Landry played for what NFL team?

A. New York Giants.

———◆———

Q. Where was the first recorded rodeo held in Texas?
A. Pecos (July 4, 1883).

———◆———

Q. Singer Jim Reeves was drafted by what major league club while playing baseball at the University of Texas?

A. St. Louis Cardinals.

Q. Fairfield hosts what September championship event?

A. Texas State Coon Hunt Championship.

———◆———

Q. Which schools shared the 1986 Southwest Conference Basketball Championship?

A. TCU, Texas, and Texas A&M.

———◆———

Q. Football great Sammy Baugh was born in what Texas town?

A. Sweetwater.

———◆———

Q. Shamrock is the home of what beauty pageant?

A. Miss Irish Rose coronation.

———◆———

Q. Garland is home for what modern softball facility?

A. Jerry Carter Softball Complex.

———◆———

Q. Roger Staubach was elected to the Pro Football Hall of Fame in what year?

A. 1985.

———◆———

Q. What Houston Rocket set an NBA record with 78 consecutive free throws?

A. Calvin Murphy.

Q. Byron Nelson and Ben Hogan both worked as caddies at what Fort Worth golf course?

A. Glen Garden Country Club.

———◆———

Q. Who has served as chief talent scout of the Dallas Cowboys since the team's formation in 1960?

A. Gil Brandt.

———◆———

Q. What San Antonio Spurs player was the NBA scoring leader for four seasons, 1977–80 and 1981–82?

A. George Gervin.

———◆———

Q. What is the oldest winery in Texas?

A. Val Verde Winery, Del Rio.

———◆———

Q. Texas Sports Hall of Fame member Arthur ("Pinkey") Whitney continues to hold the third base fielding records for what teams?

A. Philadelphia Phillies and Boston Braves.

———◆———

Q. Where on June 24, 1932, was the first jack rabbit roping contest in Texas held?

A. Odessa.

———◆———

Q. For what university did Pro Football Hall of Famer Clyde ("Bulldog") Turner play prior to his years with the Chicago Bears?

A. Hardin-Simmons.

Q. What Texas-born moundsman has topped all pitchers for lifetime strikeouts in major league play?

A. Nolan Ryan.

———◆———

Q. What four SMU players have been inducted into the Pro Football Hall of Fame?

A. Lamar Hunt (1972), Raymond Berry (1973), Forest Gregg (1977), and Doak Walker (1986).

———◆———

Q. How many times has Texas-born Willie Shoemaker won the Kentucky Derby?

A. Four.

———◆———

Q. The Houston Astrodome celebrated its Grand Opening on what date?

A. April 9, 1965.

———◆———

Q. Who served Coach Dana X. Bible as the original Twelfth Man at Texas A&M?

A. Dr. E. King Gill.

———◆———

Q. What minor league player was so popular in Houston that a candy bar named the "Ducky-Wucky Bar" was sold during the games?

A. Joe ("Ducky") Medwick.

———◆———

Q. Who was the first native Texan ever to win the British Open?

A. Ben Hogan.

SPORTS & LEISURE

Q. What trophy is awarded to the victor of the annual Texas–Oklahoma football game?

A. The Golden Hat Award.

◆

Q. In 1970 what Houston golfer beat Lee Trevino by one stroke in the Colonial National Invitational at Fort Worth?

A. Homero Blancas.

◆

Q. At what Hondo attraction can exotic game such as axis and Indian blackbuck antelope be hunted year round?

A. 777 Exotic Game Ranch.

◆

Q. Where are the Border Olympics held?
A. Laredo.

◆

Q. Cowboy fans honored what tackle as their "Favorite Cowboy" in 1983?

A. Jim Cooper.

◆

Q. What is the state dish of Texas?
A. Chili.

◆

Q. What Abilene Christian senior set a national record in the outdoor pole vault in 1982?

A. Billy Olson (18 feet, 8¾ inches).

Q. During his college career, Tom Landry won All-Southwest Conference honors his junior year playing what positions?

A. Fullback and defensive back.

———◆———

Q. Having secured four national titles and a Gold Medal in the Pan-American Games, what Austin resident was known as the "Dean of American Bicycle Road Racers"?

A. John Howard.

———◆———

Q. Rice University first became the host of what bowl game in 1959?

A. Bluebonnet Bowl.

———◆———

Q. What is the name of the 17-story parachute drop at Six Flags Over Texas?

A. Texas Chute-Out.

———◆———

Q. SMU basketball annually presents what accolade for Most Improved Player?

A. Doc Hayes Award.

———◆———

Q. The town of Orange hosts what gourmet contest the first weekend in May?

A. The International Gumbo Cookoff.

———◆———

Q. What former Houston Oiler holds the record for most career touchdowns with 73?

A. Earl Campbell.

Q. On January 1, 1937, how many fans attended the first Cotton Bowl, played by Texas Christian University and Marquette?

A. 17,000.

Q. What world welterweight wrestling champion of the 1920s established Boys Ranch in 1939?

A. Cal Farley.

Q. In the early days of SMU football, what nickname was given the team due to its having so many theological students on the squad?

A. "The Parsons."

Q. What two Houston Oilers have been inducted into the Pro Football Hall of Fame?

A. George Blanda and Ken Houston.

Q. In 1976 what Texas school sent the first American team to Europe to play exhibition football games?

A. Texas A&I University at Kingsville.

Q. Medieval Europe comes alive in what fall event staged at Plantersville?

A. The Texas Renaissance Festival.

Q. Who was the first Texas Leaguer to be recognized as the Most Valuable Player in the majors?

A. Dizzy Dean.

Q. What community boasts the highest golf course in Texas?

A. Marfa.

Q. What Bonham-born Cincinnati Reds infielder set the National League record for most double plays by a shortstop (129) during the 1954 season?

A. Roy McMillan.

Q. What Texas Sports Hall of Fame member was a two-time All-American at Texas Tech and a lineman for the Kansas City Chiefs in Super Bowl I?

A. E. J. Holub.

Q. Rogers Hornsby was born in what Texas town?

A. Winters.

Q. What two Texas Rangers players showed up at a 1982 game wearing paper bags over their heads?

A. Larry Parrish and Doc Medich.

Q. What Texas Ranger manager marked up a perfect record of 1.000 for his major league managerial career?

A. Del Wilber, who managed only one game.

Q. The baseball facility at the University of Texas is named after what two legendary Longhorn coaches?

A. Billy Disch and Bibb Falk.

Q. Of what Houston golfer did Arnold Palmer say, "He could play piano all night and shoot 65 the next day"?

A. Jimmy Demaret.

---◆---

Q. Who became the Dallas Cowboys' first ever first-round NFL college draft choice?

A. Ed ("Too Tall") Jones (1974).

---◆---

Q. Curt Flood played 12 years with the St. Louis Cardinals at what position?

A. Center field.

---◆---

Q. Mexican rodeos held along the Texas-Mexico border are known by what name?

A. Charredas.

---◆---

Q. In what community is the International Kite Museum?

A. Corpus Christi.

---◆---

Q. What Goliad track is known for Quarter Horse racing?

A. La Bahia Downs.

---◆---

Q. While playing with the Oakland A's, what Austin-born line drive hitter was second only to Carl Yastrzemski in American League batting?

A. Danny Cater.

Q. According to legend, the term *bullpen* was first used in Austin under what circumstances?

A. The pitchers were warming up in an area near a Bull Durham Tobacco sign.

Q. What was the first professional golf tournament hosted by the city of Dallas?

A. The $10,000 Texas Victory Open (1944).

Q. At what high school was David Greig Browning, Jr., state diving champion three times?

A. Dallas Highland Park.

Q. SMU home basketball games are played in what arena?

A. Moody Coliseum.

Q. What was presented to baseball coach Bibb Falk upon his retirement from the University of Texas in 1967?

A. 476 cigars, one for each victory.

Q. Who became Rice University's basketball career scoring leader with 1,847 points at the end of his college career in 1982?

A. Ricky Pierce.

Q. Waco-born Lynwood ("Schoolboy") Rowe pitched in the 1934, 1935, and 1940 World Series for what major league team?

A. Detroit Tigers.

Q. Chicago fans gave native Texan Ernie Banks what honorary title?

A. "Mr. Chicago Cub."

Q. What Texas swimming facility was the site of the 1980 Olympic Trials?

A. The Texas Swimming Center, University of Texas.

Q. The Houston Oilers have retired the jerseys of what two players?

A. Jim Norton (#43) and Elvin Bethea (#65).

Q. What former SMU player was awarded the Heisman Trophy in 1948?

A. Doak Walker.

Q. In May of 1982 what Richardson resident became the winningest LPGA golfer in history?

A. Kathy Whitworth.

Q. What Bonita-born Yankee pitcher hit his only major league home run in 1927, causing Babe Ruth to fall off the bench in astonishment?

A. Wilcy ("Cy") Moore.

Q. What Lufkin festival held in May highlights a southern tradition?

A. Southern Hushpuppy Olympics.

Q. What baseball executive, formerly a Texas Leaguer, established the farm system?

A. Branch Rickey.

◆

Q. What five-foot, seven-inch Texas native plays basketball for the Atlanta Hawks?

A. Spud Webb.

◆

Q. Who was credited with being the "father of soccer" in Texas?

A. A. ("Pop") Ramsden.

◆

Q. What uniquely combined culinary/sporting event is held the first part of September in Paris?

A. The Chili du Paree Chili Cookoff & Cow Pasture Olympics.

◆

Q. What former University of Houston Cougar led the NBA in rebounding in 1970 and 1974?

A. Elvin Hayes.

◆

Q. Houston Oiler Ray Childress was named to First Team All-American honors while playing for what university?

A. Texas A&M.

◆

Q. What Texas Ranger was named Most Valuable Player of the American League in 1974?

A. Jeff Burroughs.

Q. What El Paso-born jockey won the Kentucky Derby in 1986 on a horse named Ferdinand?

A. Willie Shoemaker.

———◆———

Q. Paseo del Rey Feo, Battle of Flowers Parade, and Fiesta Flambeau are all part of what exciting and colorful celebration?

A. Fiesta San Antonio.

———◆———

Q. What Houston-born infielder played in the 1979 World Series for the Pittsburgh Pirates?

A. Phil Garner.

———◆———

Q. Where was golfer Don January born?

A. Plainview.

———◆———

Q. University of Houston halfback Bobby Brezina played for what NFL team?

A. Houston Oilers.

———◆———

Q. In 1975 what Texan was the first black golfer to play in the Masters?

A. Lee Elder.

———◆———

Q. What Texan is recognized by baseball historians as the sport's first great relief pitcher?

A. Fred Marberry.

Q. Batting .424, who set the record for highest batting average of all time in 1924?

A. Rogers Hornsby.

———————◆———————

Q. What TCU coach produced such All-Americans as Davey O'Brien, Sammy Baugh, Ki Aldrich and Darrell Lester?

A. L. R. ("Dutch") Meyer.

———————◆———————

Q. What golfing coach gave the University of Houston Cougars 12 NCAA team titles in 15 years?

A. Dave Williams.

———————◆———————

Q. Humble is home to what uniquely named festival?

A. "Good Oil Day."

———————◆———————

Q. What rare specimen was bagged near Snyder by buffalo hunter J. Wright Mooar on October 7, 1878?

A. An albino buffalo.

———————◆———————

Q. Who became the first Dallas Cowboy player to rush for more than 6,000 yards?

A. Don Perkins.

———————◆———————

Q. What Beaumont-born major league player was the first to win the Most Valuable Player Award in both the National League (1961) and American League (1966)?

A. Frank Robinson.

Q. Under what football coach did Texas Christian win its first SWC title?

A. Francis Schmidt.

———◆———

Q. How many gold medals did San Benito track star Bobby Morrow win in the 1956 Olympics?

A. Three.

———◆———

Q. Major league catcher Matt Batts was born in what city?

A. San Antonio.

———◆———

Q. Who was the only native Texan to pitch in the majors during the 1953 season?

A. Bill Henry.

———◆———

Q. What former TCU gridiron great became a football legend coaching Ole Miss to 18 bowl appearances?

A. Johnny Vaught.

———◆———

Q. In what city is the LPGA Hall of Fame?

A. Sugar Land.

———◆———

Q. Where may one participate in the annual Prairie Dog Chili Cookoff and Pickled Quail Egg Eating Championships?

A. Grand Prairie.

Q. What quarterback led the Dallas Cowboys to their first NFL Championship game?

A. Don Meredith.

———◆———

Q. Major league outfielder Sammy West was born in what Texas community?

A. Longview.

———◆———

Q. What Granger-born major league pitcher was credited with originating the "shine ball"?

A. David ("Dauntless Dave") Danforth.

———◆———

Q. Laredo encourages friendly relations between the United States and Mexico with what annual four-day fiesta?

A. The George Washington Birthday Celebration.

———◆———

Q. In 1986 what magazine called Texas the "basketball capital of the world"?

A. *Time*.

———◆———

Q. SMU's 1986 leading scorer Kevin Lewis was selected by what pro team in the sixth round of the NBA draft?

A. San Antonio Spurs.

———◆———

Q. What noted Fort Worth race car driver became the first Indy competitor to win two races from the pole position?

A. Johnny Rutherford.

Q. Where in April of 1936 was the first Rattlesnake Derby held?

A. McCamey.

———◆———

Q. Second baseman Joe Morgan played in the 1983 World Series for what major league club?

A. Philadelphia Phillies.

———◆———

Q. What SWC football coach has led the most teams (10) into the Cotton Bowl?

A. Darrell Royal.

———◆———

Q. What member of the Texas Sports Hall of Fame served as General Manager of the Houston Astros from 1962 to 1965?

A. Paul Richards.

———◆———

Q. In 1982 what Baylor University basketball star became the top scorer in the SWC with 2,130 points?

A. Terry Teagle.

———◆———

Q. Where is the annual Buccaneer Days celebration held?

A. Corpus Christi.

———◆———

Q. Crawfish races are a part of what Bridge City celebration?

A. The Saltwater Crab and Crawfish Festival.

Q. Where was pitching great Nolan Ryan born?

A. Refugio.

———◆———

Q. What term referred to the famous swing of Texas golfer Byron Nelson?

A. "Rocking chair."

———◆———

Q. In 1985 what Dallas Cowboy became the sixth NFL player in history to rush for 10,000 career yards?

A. Tony Dorsett.

———◆———

Q. What Lufkin-born Boston Red Sox infielder won the American League batting crown in 1960 and again in 1962?

A. Pete Runnels.

———◆———

Q. The Boom Town Blowout celebration is held in what town?

A. Burkburnett.

———◆———

Q. What Texas A & M linebacker was called the "Quiet Avenger" for his ferocious but gentlemanly play?

A. Aaron Wallace.

———◆———

Q. The only world championship soaring competition staged in the United States was held over the mountain peaks of what community?

A. Marfa.

Q. What 1938 TCU quarterback won the Camp, Heisman, and Maxwell Trophies all in the same year?

A. David O'Brien.

———◆———

Q. Galveston-born Gus Mancuso played his major league career at what position?

A. Catcher.

———◆———

Q. Where was the first golf course built in Texas?

A. Galveston Country Club.

———◆———

Q. What defensive back for the Houston Oilers set a career NFL record of nine touchdowns scored on interceptions?

A. Ken Houston.

———◆———

Q. In April of 1975 Vincent Hayden Hurley of Fort Worth became the National Individual Lady Champion of what sport?

A. Fencing.

———◆———

Q. Josey's World Championship Junior Barrel Races are held in what city?

A. Marshall.

———◆———

Q. Sixteenth-century England is re-created in what spring-time festival near Waxahachie?

A. Scarborough Faire.

Q. What city is the home base for the Goodyear blimp *America*?

A. Spring.

———◆———

Q. Paris-born outfielder Dave Philley was a member of what major league club when he played in the 1954 World Series?

A. Cleveland Indians.

———◆———

Q. In what Erath County community was golfing great Ben Hogan born?

A. Dublin.

———◆———

Q. In January of 1982 SMU head football coach Ron Meyers announced he was leaving to accept the head coaching position with what NFL team?

A. New England Patriots.

———◆———

Q. What community is host to the Wild Hog Cookoff and LaSalle County Fair?

A. Cotulla.

———◆———

Q. How many grand slams did Ernie Banks hit during his major league career?

A. Twelve.

———◆———

Q. Who was the first major leaguer to hit a home run in the Houston Astrodome?

A. Mickey Mantle (in an exhibition game against Houston in 1965).

Q. What Linden-born major leaguer played in the 1969, 1970, and 1971 World Series for the Baltimore Orioles?

A. Don Buford.

———◆———

Q. The Texas League of Professional Baseball Clubs was founded in what year?

A. 1888.

———◆———

Q. Parades, a carnival, fun, and food for all combine to form what Eagle Pass celebration?

A. International Friendship Festival.

———◆———

Q. What Texas Longhorn received the Outland Trophy in 1965?

A. Tommy Nobis.

———◆———

Q. Indy 500 champ Johnny Rutherford is known by what nickname?

A. "Lone Star J. R."

———◆———

Q. What Paris-born first baseman led the American League in putouts in 1951?

A. Eddie Robinson.

———◆———

Q. In what city is the Texas state fair held?

A. Dallas.

Q. What Bangs-born Pittsburgh Pirate outfielder took the National League batting championship in 1940?

A. Debs Garms.

———◆———

Q. What city is known as the "Balloon Capital of Texas"?

A. Plano.

———◆———

Q. Where did SMU's Eric Dickerson rank in the 1982 vote for the Heisman Trophy?

A. Third.

———◆———

Q. How many National League batting titles did Rogers Hornsby win during his major league career?

A. Seven.

———◆———

Q. What Dallas fighter won the World Boxing Association's welterweight title in 1966?

A. Curtis Cokes.

———◆———

Q. Major league shortstop Everett LaMar Bridges was known by what nickname?

A. "Rocky."

———◆———

Q. At what Texas college was Jess Neely head football coach for 27 seasons?

A. Rice University (1940–66).

Q. What Texarkana-born third baseman was named to the National League All-Star teams nine times?

A. Eddie Mathews (1953, 1955–62).

———◆———

Q. Born in LaRue, what 13-year veteran outfielder hit .302 with 1,357 hits in 1,222 games?

A. Carl Reynolds.

———◆———

Q. What Arlington native was the 1962 Indy Rookie of the Year?

A. Jim McElreath.

———◆———

Q. John David Crow received the 1957 Heisman Trophy while playing halfback for what school?

A. Texas A&M.

———◆———

Q. What Greenville-born rookie moundsman pitched a no-hitter for the Chicago Cubs in the second game of the 1972 season?

A. Burt Carlton Hooton.

———◆———

Q. What NFL team drafted famous first baseman Norm Cash upon graduation from college?

A. Chicago Bears.

———◆———

Q. San Antonio-born pitcher Joe Horlen played for what major league clubs?

A. Chicago White Sox and Oakland A's.

Q. What San Antonio-born baseball player set the American League record for most assists (7) by a first baseman in an extra-inning game in 1949?

A. Ferris Fain.

———◆———

Q. Texas Sports Hall of Fame member Eddie Dyer became manager of what National League ball club in 1946?

A. St. Louis Cardinals.

———◆———

Q. What SMU breaststroke champion has claimed three world records and won the gold medal at the 1983 U.S. National Festival?

A. Steve Lundquist.

———◆———

Q. Where is the annual Texas Dogwood Trails Festival held?
A. Palestine.

———◆———

Q. What Comanche-born moundsman pitched a no-hitter for the Brooklyn Dodgers against Cincinnati in 1940?

A. James ("Tex") Carleton.

———◆———

Q. For what team did Frank Robinson become the first black manager in major league history in 1975?

A. Cleveland Indians.

———◆———

Q. Elgin-born Ray Culp played what position during his major league career?

A. Pitcher.

Q. What competitors met in the first recorded baseball game played in Texas?

A. The Stonewalls of Houston and the Robert E. Lees of Galveston (1867).

──────◆──────

Q. Major league pitcher Fred Norman was born in what city?

A. San Antonio.

──────◆──────

Q. Harlingen is the home of what April celebration?

A. RioFest.

──────◆──────

Q. What Dallas Cowboy linebacker was selected Most Valuable Player in Super Bowl V?

A. Chuck Howley.

──────◆──────

Q. After serving as vice-president of the Houston Astros, what Beaumont native became coach under Leo Durocher in 1973?

A. Grady Hatton, Jr.

──────◆──────

Q. What triple-deck paddle wheeler offers daily cruises of Galveston Bay and port?

A. *The Colonel.*

──────◆──────

Q. What 1932 Odessa roping contest was revived in 1977 and blocked by court order in 1978?

A. Jackrabbit Roping Contest.

Q. What Houston Astro moundsman claimed his 250th victory in July of 1982?

A. Don Sutton.

———◆———

Q. What Hallettsville festivity features Czech and German food, music, and dancing?

A. South Texas Polka and Sausage Festival.

———◆———

Q. From 1955 to 1962 the Boston Red Sox were managed by what Texas-born major leaguer?

A. Michael ("Pinky") Higgins.

———◆———

Q. What Weatherford-born Chicago Cub pitched the only game in history in which both pitchers had a no-hitter for nine innings, only to lose to Reds pitcher Fred Toney in the tenth?

A. James Leslie ("Hippo") Vaughn.

———◆———

Q. What is the official name of the Houston Astrodome?

A. The Harris County Domed Stadium.

———◆———

Q. Dallas-born catcher Dave Duncan played in the 1972 World Series for what American League team?

A. Oakland A's.

———◆———

Q. What is the home court of the Dallas Mavericks?

A. Reunion Arena.

SCIENCE & NATURE

C H A P T E R   S I X

Q. The Yellow Rose Ranch near Odessa is the state's largest facility handling what kind of livestock?

A. Ostriches.

———◆———

Q. At their peak, how many buffalo were estimated to have existed in Texas?

A. 60,000,000 head.

———◆———

Q. What rare cactus is known as "dry whiskey"?

A. Peyote.

———◆———

Q. Coming in at 100,000 barrels a day on January 10, 1901, what Texas oil well near Beaumont is considered the "world's greatest gusher"?

A. Spindletop.

———◆———

Q. What Cleveland establishment sells more than 2,000 varieties of herbs and serves herbal meals?

A. Hilltop Country Inn.

Q. What Texas zoo was the first in the nation to create a replica of a rain forest?

A. Fort Worth Zoological Park.

◆

Q. Commercially, what is the most important tree in Texas?

A. Pine.

◆

Q. What distance does the Red River flow through or along the border of Texas?

A. 640 miles.

◆

Q. Who was the notorious early 1900s bare-handed wolf hunter from the Sherman area?

A. Jack Abernathy.

◆

Q. What Texas county ranks the highest in agricultural production?

A. Hidalgo.

◆

Q. With approximately 38,000 feet of mapped passages, what is the longest cave in Texas?

A. Powell's Cave (Menard County).

◆

Q. The state's largest active sand dune field is in what state park?

A. Monahans Sandhills State Park.

Q. The lechuzilla and sotel cactus were used by prehistoric Texans as a source for what?

A. Material for weaving.

———◆———

Q. Who was the first Texan to grow cotton commercially?

A. Jared Groce.

———◆———

Q. What is the smallest variety of cactus found in Texas?

A. Button cactus.

———◆———

Q. Where does Texas rank nationally in the production of portland cement?

A. First.

———◆———

Q. How many species of dove are found in Texas?

A. Eight.

———◆———

Q. What east Texas tree is known for its "knees"?

A. Cypress.

———◆———

Q. The nation's largest sinkhole, Devil's Sinkhole, is near what community in Edwards County?

A. Rocksprings.

Q. Located on 850 acres, what drive-through wildlife park features animals from around the world?

A. Texas Safari Wildlife Park.

---◆---

Q. What Texas wildflower is also called by such names as wolfflower, buffalo clover, and *el conejo* ("the rabbit")?

A. Bluebonnet.

---◆---

Q. Extending 110 miles, what is the longest barrier island on the Texas coast?

A. Padre Island.

---◆---

Q. Where is the largest aquarium in Texas?

A. Fair Park, Dallas.

---◆---

Q. What is the world's largest privately owned wildlife refuge?

A. Welder Wildlife Refuge, Sinton.

---◆---

Q. What is the largest spring-fed river in Texas?

A. Guadalupe River.

---◆---

Q. The white oak planted in 1977 in Austin's Symphony Square was grown from an acorn from the grounds of what famous presidential estate?

A. Mount Vernon.

Q. Who brought the first commercial shipment of nursery stock into north central Texas in 1870?

A. John M. Howell.

———————◆———————

Q. Measuring 107 feet in height, what is the highest water-fall in Texas?

A. Capote Falls (near Candelaria).

———————◆———————

Q. What is the most colorful bird indigenous to Texas?

A. The Painted Bunting.

———————◆———————

Q. What oil field discovered in 1930 is now the largest in the state?

A. The East Texas Oil Field.

———————◆———————

Q. Where is the largest rattlesnake round-up in Texas held?

A. Sweetwater.

———————◆———————

Q. Where did the state record 65 inches of snowfall in the winter of 1923–24?

A. Romero.

———————◆———————

Q. The Los Ebanos Ferry crosses the Rio Grande by what means of propulsion?

A. It is pulled by hand.

Q. In 1978 Grand Prairie resident Don Emmick constructed a miniature airplane powered by what source?

A. One housefly.

Q. Where was the last recorded Texas sighting of an ivory-billed woodpecker made in 1904?

A. Tarkington.

Q. What county has produced the most oil in Texas?

A. Gregg.

Q. What tree was determined to be the geographic center of Texas by a 1922 Federal survey team?

A. The Heart of Texas Oak.

Q. A salt dome reaching 1 1/2 miles across and approximately 16,000 feet thick lies beneath what community?

A. Grand Saline.

Q. What state park is noted for its unique botanical gardens?

A. Palmetto State Park.

Q. In 1889 the XIT Ranch introduced what breed of cattle into Texas?

A. Angus.

Q. At what museum can visitors walk under a vast sea, viewing the area as it would have been 230 million years ago?

A. The Petroleum Museum, Midland.

———◆———

Q. How many persons lost their lives to a tornado that struck Goliad on May 18, 1902?

A. 114.

———◆———

Q. Who performed the first recorded appendectomy in Texas in 1879 at Bonham?

A. Dr. Bacon Saunders.

———◆———

Q. According to the National Weather Service, what is the nation's sunniest city?

A. El Paso.

———◆———

Q. What species of armadillo is found in Texas?

A. The nine-banded armadillo.

———◆———

Q. Mission calls itself the home of what citrus fruit?

A. The Texas Ruby Red Grapefruit.

———◆———

Q. What geographical area leads Texas in wheat production?

A. The Panhandle.

Q. In recognition of its valuable spinach crop, Crystal City erected what monument?

A. A statue of Popeye the Sailor Man.

———◆———

Q. What is the largest cave system in Texas?

A. The Natural Bridge Caverns.

———◆———

Q. In 1895 what breed of cattle was introduced into Texas by Victoria resident T. B. Wood and Al McFaddin of Refugio?

A. Brahma.

———◆———

Q. How many varieties of wildflowers are found in Texas?

A. Approximately 5,300.

———◆———

Q. What mine near Shafter was the primary source of gold and silver produced in Texas?

A. Presidio mine.

———◆———

Q. The large whip scorpion commonly found in Texas is called by what other name?

A. Vinegaroon.

———◆———

Q. What was named the official Texas state bird in 1927?

A. Mockingbird.

Q. Who is credited with discovering the world-famous dinosaur tracks along the Paluxy River at Glen Rose in 1909?

A. George B. Adams.

---◆---

Q. What is the official state tree of Texas?

A. Pecan.

---◆---

Q. In 1895 the Corsicana Oil Development Company became the first oil producer to utilize what means of transportation for oil?

A. A railroad tank car.

---◆---

Q. From what Texas lake was a record 13-pound, 8-ounce largemouth bass taken in 1943 by H. R. Magee?

A. Medina Lake.

---◆---

Q. What town is the home of the only corn-wet milling plant in the southwest?

A. Dimmitt.

---◆---

Q. At what figure did Texas cattle production peak in 1906?

A. 9.5 million head.

---◆---

Q. Who founded the Texas Heart Institute in 1960?

A. Dr. Denton A. Cooley.

Q. What Texan invented the process for condensing milk?

A. Gail Borden, Jr.

———◆———

Q. In March of what year did Cascade Caverns near Boerne open as the state's first commercial cave?

A. 1932.

———◆———

Q. Where in 1900 was flax first planted in Texas?

A. Victoria.

———◆———

Q. In what county was the first geothermal well in Texas drilled in 1978?

A. Brazoria.

———◆———

Q. What heavy metal is extracted from the cinnabar mined in the Terlingua area?

A. Mercury (quicksilver).

———◆———

Q. What record-setting high temperature for Texas was set on August 12, 1936, at Seymour?

A. 120 degrees.

———◆———

Q. The unusual white-tailed deer taken by Jeff Benson in McCullough County in 1892 had how many points on its rack?

A. 78.

Q. What Wheeler-born native became the first Texan to walk on the moon in 1969?

A. Alan L. Bean.

———◆———

Q. What Texas city is known as the "cotton capital of the world"?

A. Lubbock.

———◆———

Q. Forests cover what portion of Texas?

A. Fourteen percent.

———◆———

Q. Who in 1899 became the first woman optometrist in Texas and the second in the nation?

A. Mollie Wright Armstrong.

———◆———

Q. On September 29, 1976, the Fort Worth Zoo became the second facility in the nation to successfully hatch what rare reptile?

A. Dwarf crocodiles.

———◆———

Q. Where was the first oil well in Texas drilled?

A. Near Melrose in Nacogdoches County.

———◆———

Q. In what community is the W. R. Poage Pecan Field Station, which has developed sixteen new varieties since 1953?

A. Brownwood.

Q. Wild hogs commonly called razorbacks are given what name in parts of East Texas?

A. "Piney rooters."

———◆———

Q. What is the deepest known cave in Texas?

A. Lantry Lead Cave in Val Verde County (367 feet).

———◆———

Q. "Town without a toothache" was a title given to what community because of the natural fluorides in the water supply?

A. Hereford.

———◆———

Q. What is the most common sea gull along the Texas coast?

A. Laughing gull.

———◆———

Q. What University of Texas facility was built following a bequest from amateur astronomer William J. McDonald?

A. McDonald Observatory, Mount Locke.

———◆———

Q. Uranium was first discovered in what county in 1954?

A. Karnes.

———◆———

Q. What is the largest floral event in Texas?

A. The Texas Rose Festival, Tyler.

Q. Standing seven feet tall at the shoulders, what was the name of the largest steer ever raised in Texas?

A. "First National."

———◆———

Q. In 1909, what feed store owner helped found the Humble Oil and Refining Company (now Exxon)?

A. Ross Sterling.

———◆———

Q. During the "Great Gulf Snow" in February of 1895, how much snow was dumped on Galveston during a single 24-hour period?

A. 15.4 inches.

———◆———

Q. Where was the first state forest established in 1924?

A. Newton County (the E. O. Siecke State Forest).

———◆———

Q. How many varieties of grasses grow in Texas?

A. Over 500.

———◆———

Q. Where is the largest and oldest medical school in Texas?

A. Galveston (The University of Texas Medical Branch).

———◆———

Q. Where does Texas rank nationally in the production of watermelons?

A. First.

Q. What is the most prolific cactus found in Texas?

A. Fishhook barrel cactus.

———◆———

Q. On August 19–20, 1886, what community became the only Texas town to be totally destroyed by a hurricane and never rebuilt?

A. Indianola.

———◆———

Q. In 1972 what Texas zoo became the first in the nation in which a white rhino was born?

A. San Antonio Zoo.

———◆———

Q. The record 1949 cotton crop produced how many bales?

A. Six million.

———◆———

Q. What soft carbon-based material is mined in Burnet County?

A. Graphite.

———◆———

Q. Where and when did John Z. Means and C. O. Finley kill the only grizzly bear ever taken in Texas?

A. The Davis Mountains (1890).

———◆———

Q. What four types of poisonous snakes are found in Texas?

A. Copperhead, coral, cottonmouth, and rattlesnakes.

Q. What state park is known for its large prairie dog population?

A. MacKenzie State Park.

———◆———

Q. Of the twenty-three species of ducks found in Port Arthur wildlife refuges, what is the only resident species?

A. Mottled duck.

———◆———

Q. What Houston physician and surgeon pioneered the pacemaker and developed many unique and innovative cardiovascular surgical techniques?

A. Dr. Michael DeBakey.

———◆———

Q. Who brought the first Hereford cattle into Texas in 1876?

A. Captain W. S. Ikard.

———◆———

Q. What lake that extends into Oklahoma also is the largest man-made lake in Texas?

A. Texoma.

———◆———

Q. Where was the world's first ammonia refrigerant ice plant?

A. Jefferson.

———◆———

Q. Muleshoe Wildlife Refuge is home to large numbers of what type of large crane?

A. Sandhill.

Q. In February of 1956 Hale Center set a state record for how much snowfall in a single month?

A. 36 inches.

———◆———

Q. What town is completely surrounded by the $4.4 billion superconducting supercollider?

A. Waxahachie.

———◆———

Q. In what unique Texas mammal are the litters always of the same sex?

A. Armadillo.

———◆———

Q. How does the Rio Grande River rank in length in the Western Hemisphere?

A. Ninth.

———◆———

Q. How many species of catfish are found in the waters of Texas?

A. Ten.

———◆———

Q. What is the largest national forest in Texas?

A. Sabine National Forest.

———◆———

Q. What was the first airplane to be produced at the Fort Worth Division of General Dynamics in 1942?

A. The B-24 Liberator.

Q. What is the driest region of Texas?

A. The Trans-Pecos.

Q. What French botanist conducted the first extensive study of Texas plants in 1824?

A. Dr. Luis Berlandier.

Q. How much land was needed for the development of the superconducting supercollider?

A. 16,000 acres.

Q. What Texas county is best known for topaz deposits?

A. Mason.

Q. The "Gossamer Penguin," the world's first solar-powered aircraft, is displayed at what museum?

A. The Science Place/Southwest Museum of Science and Technology in Dallas.

Q. In what year was the first commercial grapefruit grove planted in the Rio Grande Valley?

A. 1904.

Q. Internationally famous adventurer and wild animal expert Frank ("Bring 'Em Back Alive") Buck was born in what Texas town?

A. Gainesville.

Q. To what all-time record low did Texas oil prices drop in 1902?

A. Three cents a barrel.

◆

Q. Established in 1935, what is the oldest national wildlife refuge in Texas?

A. Muleshoe Wildlife Refuge.

◆

Q. What Texan invented the electrical digital watch, which he called Pulsar?

A. George Theiss.

◆

Q. What Texas town is called the "turkey capital of the world"?

A. Cuero.

◆

Q. What is the smallest poisonous snake in Texas?

A. Western pigmy rattlesnake (about eighteen inches in length).

◆

Q. What is the second most valuable crop in Texas?

A. Sorghum grain.

◆

Q. What was the weight of the state record flathead catfish pulled from Lake Livingston in 1976 by Charles J. Booth?

A. 114 pounds.

Q. What community is noted for having sealed a horned toad in the cornerstone of its courthouse in 1896, only to retrieve it alive in 1927?

A. Eastland.

------◆------

Q. In 1981, a law was passed to protect cacti from what crime?

A. Cactus rustling.

------◆------

Q. How tall do buffaloes stand at the shoulders?

A. Five and one-half to six feet.

------◆------

Q. What record cold temperature was recorded at both Tulia on February 12, 1899, and Seminole on February 8, 1933?

A. -23° fahrenheit.

------◆------

Q. Situated in Montague and Wise Counties, what is the largest national grassland in Texas?

A. Lyndon B. Johnson National Grasslands.

------◆------

Q. Who in 1949 became the first television meteorologist in Texas?

A. Harold Taft (with WBAP–TV, Fort Worth).

------◆------

Q. Where did Franciscan friars open the first silver mines in Texas in 1680?

A. The El Paso area.

Q. In 1987, what Texas Tech University professor discovered the skeleton of a *Protoavis*, Earth's oldest bird?

A. Sankar Chatterjee.

———◆———

Q. The leaves of what plant, called balmony by the early settlers, was brewed into a laxative tea by Texas pioneers?

A. Wild foxglove.

———◆———

Q. What Comal County cave presently houses the state's largest bat population?

A. Braken Bat Cave.

———◆———

Q. What community became the first to utilize natural gas for lighting and fuel in 1901?

A. Corsicana.

———◆———

Q. What is the largest game bird in Texas?
A. The wild turkey.

———◆———

Q. What wildlife program has restored the endangered red wolf to East Texas?

A. Red Wolf Recovery Program.

———◆———

Q. What ranks as the most valuable product in Texas?
A. Petroleum.

Q. What Mission native was known as the father of the Texas citrus industry?

A. John H. Shary.

———◆———

Q. How many species of birds are found in Texas?

A. Over 540.

———◆———

Q. What Panhandle quarries provided highly-prized flint for the Paleolithic peoples of Texas?

A. The Alibates Flint Quarries.

———◆———

Q. Near the San Bernard River at Eagle Lake, 3,400 acres have been set aside as a refuge for what type fowl?

A. Attwater Prairie Chicken.

———◆———

Q. The nation's largest reserve of what lighter-than-air gas is found in the Texas Panhandle?

A. Helium.

———◆———

Q. Where is the "Big Tree," the largest in Texas?

A. Goose Island State Park, Rockport.

———◆———

Q. What is the leading source of farm income in Texas?

A. Beef cattle.

Q. In 1971 what grass became the official state grass of Texas?

A. Sideoats gama.

Q. What Texas zoo is noted for maintaining the state's largest collection of endangered animal species?

A. Brownsville's Gladys Porter Zoo.

Q. Who brought the first cattle into Texas in 1541?

A. Francisco Vasquez de Coronado.

Q. During a freak storm on March 1, 1973, what substance piled up 6 to 24 inches deep on Interstate 45 near Conroe?

A. Hailstones.

Q. What Texan became world-famous as an oil well fire fighter?

A. Paul ("Red") Adair.

Q. Near what community are the largest asphalt deposits in Texas found?

A. Uvalde.

Q. What native of San Antonio was the first Texan to fly and to walk in space?

A. Edward H. White II.

Q. What type of communication system was established between Fort Worth and Dallas in 1874?

A. Telegraph.

———◆———

Q. Who brought the first ginkgo tree to Tyler in 1889?

A. Ambassador Richard Bennett Hubbard.

———◆———

Q. Who is known as the "Father of Texas Agriculture"?

A. Jared Groce.

———◆———

Q. Pecos is known nationally for producing what delicious melon?

A. Pecos cantaloupe.

———◆———

Q. How many national parks are within Texas?

A. Two (Big Bend National Park and Guadalupe Mountains National Park).

———◆———

Q. In what year was helium production begun in Texas?

A. 1918.

———◆———

Q. In what state park is a 40,000-acre forest of miniature oak trees?

A. Monahans Sandhills State Park.

Q. Found in Culberson and Hudspeth Counties, what is the softest mineral in the state?

A. Talc.

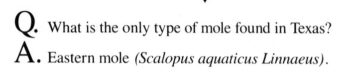

Q. What is the only type of mole found in Texas?

A. Eastern mole *(Scalopus aquaticus Linnaeus)*.

Q. Who drilled the first oil well in Texas in 1866?

A. Lyne T. Barret.

Q. What is the record measurement—tip to tip—for a set of Texas Longhorn horns?

A. 8 feet, 9 inches.

Q. The Comal Springs at New Braunfels averages how many cubic feet of water per minute?

A. 18,180.

Q. What San Antonio Zoo specimen was featured in the movie *The Deep?*

A. A green moray eel.

Q. Where was the first uranium processing plant constructed in Texas in 1961?

A. Deweesville.

Q. With more than 400 archeological sites, what county is one of the richest areas in the nation in aboriginal cave paintings?

A. Val Verde.

———◆———

Q. What Culberson County mine was the leading producer of copper in Texas?

A. Hazel mine.

———◆———

Q. In what city is the Rexene Company, the largest petrochemical complex in the inland United States?

A. Odessa.

———◆———

Q. Who at the University of Texas Southwestern Medical School in Dallas performed the first successful kidney transplant in the state in 1963?

A. Dr. Paul Peter.

———◆———

Q. What is the official stone of Texas?

A. Fossilized palm wood.

———◆———

Q. How many horses were rounded up in 1878 in Texas's largest ever single wild mustang round-up?

A. 1,000 head.

———◆———

Q. Where were the first orange seeds planted in Texas in 1872?

A. Laguna Seca Ranch near Mission.

Q. What is the most endangered variety of amphibians in Texas?

A. The Houston toad.

Q. Laredo has the only smelter in Texas for processing what material from the mineral stibnite?

A. Antimony.

Q. Where is the Scientific Balloon Base, operated by NASA?

A. Palestine.

Q. Where does Texas rank nationally in production of grapefruit?

A. Second.

Q. At their peak, how many producing oil wells were within the city limits of Kilgore?

A. 1,000.

Q. What is considered to be the largest recorded hurricane to hit the Texas coast?

A. Hurricane Carla (1961).

Q. Where on April 28, 1978, was a funeral held for "Big Al," a 12-foot alligator?

A. Lone Star.

Q. What Grand Champion stallion from the King Ranch became the first horse to be registered by the American Quarter Horse Association?

A. "Wimpy," P-1.

———◆———

Q. Where in Texas did the Federal government construct a tin smelter?

A. Texas City.

———◆———

Q. Large deposits of multi-colored petrified wood gave what community its name?

A. Palo Pinto ("painted post").

———◆———

Q. What is the largest canyon in Texas?

A. Palo Duro Canyon.

———◆———

Q. Including its tributary, the Pecos, how large is the Rio Grande River drainage area?

A. 48,475 square miles.

———◆———

Q. Who became the first cattleman to successfully cross breed Brahmas and native stock in 1874?

A. Captain Mifflin Kenedy.

———◆———

Q. In 1868 where was the first oil pipeline laid in Texas?

A. Near Chireno.

Q. What is the highest mountain in Texas?

A. Guadalupe Peak, also called Signal Peak (8,751 feet above sea level).

———◆———

Q. What two types of vultures are found in Texas?

A. Black and turkey.

———◆———

Q. Where in Nacogdoches County was the state's first elementary oil refinery constructed in 1888?

A. Oil Springs.

———◆———

Q. What town was the site of the most elaborate rainmaking experiments in the United States?

A. Post.

———◆———

Q. The Rio Grande was first given what name by the early Spanish explorer Alonso Alvarez de Pineda?

A. Rio de las Palmas.

———◆———

Q. In what county in 1911 was the state's only authenticated gem-quality diamond found?

A. Foard.

———◆———

Q. The state's best farmland is in which land region?

A. North-Central Plains.

Q. What record number of oil wells were drilled in Texas in 1956?

A. 13,082.

Q. What scientist authenticated the remains of the Midland Man, which proved the existence of man in the Midland area 22,000 years ago?

A. Dr. Fred Wendorf.

Q. In what Texas river is quicksand most plentiful?

A. Canadian River.

Q. What company pioneered the technique of using super-heated water to mine sulphur in Texas in 1912?

A. The Freeport Sulphur Company.

Q. How many tornadoes were spawned across Texas by the effects of Hurricane Beulah on September 20, 1967?

A. 67.

Q. What is the only egg-laying poisonous snake in Texas?

A. Coral snake.

Q. What company pioneered long distance gas pipelines in the state in 1909?

A. Lone Star.

Q. What is the height of the unique underground waterfall in Cascade Caverns?

A. 90 feet.

━━━━◆━━━━

Q. What Odessa landmark, formed 20,000 years ago, is the second largest in the United States and the sixth largest in the world?

A. Odessa Meteor Crater.

━━━━◆━━━━

Q. What type of cattle developed on the King Ranch did the U.S. Department of Agriculture list as the first distinctive American beef cattle breed?

A. Santa Gertrudis.

━━━━◆━━━━

Q. In what city is the world's largest grapefruit juice canning plant?

A. Weslaco.

━━━━◆━━━━

Q. In what central Texas river are freshwater pearls ranging in color from pink to purple found?

A. Concho River.

━━━━◆━━━━

Q. What San Antonio-born researcher performed some of the earliest extensive studies on the role of bats in insect control?

A. Charles A. R. Campbell.

━━━━◆━━━━

Q. Where is the only known nesting place of the Colima warbler in the United States?

A. Big Bend National Park.

Q. How many varieties of goldenrod are found in Texas?

A. Over thirty.

◆

Q. What three types of blind snakes are found in Texas?

A. Plains, New Mexico, and Trans-Pecos.

◆

Q. What unique variety of pink granite found only in Texas is noted for an interspersing of sky-blue quartz crystals?

A. Llanite.

◆

Q. What Texas agency plants the most wildflowers in the state?

A. The State Department of Highways and Public Works.

◆

Q. Measuring some three and one-half miles by one and one-half miles, where is the largest outcropping of Texas serpentine in the state?

A. The Coal Creek mass in Blanco and Gillespie counties.

◆

Q. In 1961, what university donated most of the land to NASA on which the Manned Spacecraft Center was to be constructed?

A. Rice University.

◆

Q. Where is the national headquarters of the American Poinsettia Society?

A. Mission.